CATCHING PARADISE IN HAWAI'I

WINSTON CONRAD

Some of the names and identities of the islanders have been changed to protect their privacy.

Published by Quill
An Inkshares Collection, Oakland, California
www.inkshares.com

Cover painting by Harry Wishard
Book design by Blue Design, Inc. (www.bluedes.com)

ISBN: 9781947848702

First edition

Printed in the United States of America

FOR WILL JAMES

Away out there in the mid-solitudes of the vast Pacific, and far down in the edge of the tropics, they lie asleep on the waves, perpetually green and beautiful, remote from the work-day world and its frets and worries, a bloomy, fragrant paradise, where the troubled may go and find peace, and the sick and tired find strength and rest. There they lie, the divine islands, forever shining in the sun, forever smiling out on the sparkling sea . . .

—MARK TWAIN, FROM AN UNFINISHED NOVEL, 1884

CONTENTS

CHAPTER ONE

Arriving In Paradise

Keep true to the dreams of thy youth.
—A MOTTO BY FRIEDRICH VON SCHILLER, 1800, WAS PINNED
TO THE LID OF HERMAN MELVILLE'S WRITING BOX.

Fishing shack, love shack, is what distracted me. I hopped, hissed, and groaned, dripping blood on the weathered planks and tiles. Valerie offered me a Kleenex and said, "You'd have to add a little *aloha* to this place."

"Sure, it's old; over fifty years ago, they built these plantation cottages," said Woody. He randomly poked the walls of the art studio with a knife and added casually, "And plenty of termites."

"Termites?" A sinking feeling rolled into my stomach. I glanced at my wife, Paulette, who looked back.

"Damage isn't *that* bad." Woody, the middle-aged inspector, had come to the islands from Colorado twenty years ago, joined the Kona Canoe Club, and stayed. "Of course, you've heard the saying 'If the termites behind the walls stop holding hands, the whole building will fall down.'" He laughed, but I didn't. My wife and I were thinking of buying this house, but now . . .

My toe was killing me. On the way down the steps, I had cut my sandaled foot on a chipped loose blue tile, and it had skidded—*bloop*—into the pond.

The old wooden floor and the redwood plank walls added warmth to the art studio. Green oxidation dotted the old bronze fan blades that barely stirred the air, stale with a South Seas humidity that reminded me of a scene out of Somerset Maugham's story "Rain."

"Is the building worth saving?" I asked.

"Better than most of the ol' shacks I see down here," said Woody.

He added that a few of the deck pilings over the pond needed repair and that the structure sloped to one side, but it was habitable. "We're probably below sea level, but heck—that doesn't seem to bother the Dutch."

Valerie Kale, the blonde realtor, was a *haole* (a Caucasian) and a *kamaʻāina*, a native of the islands. Standing close by was her twelve-year-old daughter, who had long dark hair and both Hawaiian and Caucasian features, one of that handsome race known as *hapa*, half. (Families that have married completely within their own ethnic groups are now the exception in Hawaiʻi, not the rule.)

I asked Valerie about disclosures.

"Well," she said.

"Yes?"

"There is a rodent issue."

"Issue," I echoed. "Rats?"

And then the coup de grâce. "There sure is!" piped in a female voice from nowhere, with a southern drawl.

The busty redheaded renter, Susanna, sashayed in from the beach in a bikini and a towel wrapped around her waist. "One night I woke up and a rat was nibbling on my arm. Bit me right here," she said, lifting a mottled forearm.

In a corner, debris was hanging from the ceiling. Woody fetched a ladder and confirmed that it was, indeed, part of a rat's nest. Stains marked where the roof leaked. On the other side of the studio, we found a dozen dead centipedes—one six inches long—as well as three dead scorpions.

"They crawl in under the bathroom door at night," chirped Susanna. "This place has some *real* problems. However, we'd be happy to look after it for y'all, How long a lease can we have? The other people who were gonna buy this place promised us three years. How 'bout y'all?" Blanche DuBois on bummer acid. I ignored her to focus on the work—an immense undertaking if we actually bought the place.

"A little paint and putty, be right fine little love nest for ya," Woody said, smiling.

"Let's see the main house," Valerie said, clearing her throat.

"Main's fine." Woody clomped across the rotten boards of the porch in his work boots and waved. "Aloha."

"It's an interesting story, how the architect built this *magnificent* place next to the old fishing shack," Valerie said as she led Paulette and me out of the studio.

We followed her through the overgrown yard, past the koi pond, to the main house. It was modern and solidly set on concrete pillars over the rear portion of the brackish pond. Inside, dust filled our nostrils. It did not augur well.

"I guess the house cleaners didn't show up." Valerie apologized as we climbed the stairs to the large bedroom loft. "But the owner is a nice old man."

The bedroom fan scattered dust and a few dead insects when Valerie turned it on. Behind a bug-spattered white plastic strip curtain, a large sliding glass door led out onto a balcony from which, through an opening in the dense jungle brush, one could see patches of red dirt with tan grass, small kiawe[1] trees, and a vast desert beyond. Behind that, the hills undulated, eventually forming the slopes of high volcanic mountains.

"Kohala Mountain is the oldest volcano on the island. It has been extinct for sixty thousand years," Valerie recited. "Of course, there in front of us is Mauna Kea, the highest peak in the Pacific at 13,796 feet. From the ocean floor to the top, it rises over six miles." To its right stretched a massive dome, its top dusted white with snow.

"That's Mauna Loa, which means 'Long Mountain,'" said Valerie.

Fifty miles across and as high as the Alps, it is the biggest sea mountain on Earth. Its volcanic eruptions created one-sixth of the island of Hawai'i, which is roughly the size of Connecticut.

"And if you trim back those trees, you can just barely make out Hualalai Mountain," Valerie said.

We stretched our necks to get a glimpse of the poetic sounding "Who-ah-la-lie." We saw nothing but trees and brush. "Uh, hmm," said Paulette and I in unison; views alone would not entice us to buy this place. There was something fishy about this old dog.

Below us was a figure-eight-shaped pond with a little wooden bridge spanning the waist. On a small island, four feet in diameter, sprouted a lone coconut palm whose trunk bore a plywood sign with the crudely lettered words "Gilligan's Island" painted on it. Secretly, an island was actually what I wanted: a place of savage beauty where I could hide away, recharge my batteries, and in the process, find

---

1. *Kiawe (Prosopis pallida) is an algaroba tree from Peru, first planted in Hawai'i in 1828 as shade for cattle. It grows profusely in the dry areas of Hawai'i and makes for excellent firewood for cooking. However, its thorns are vicious and can poke through tennis shoes and rubber tires.*

tranquility from modern grit—a sort of electronic nightmare. I stared at that pathetic circle of land in the pond, a miniscule island within the larger one of Hawai'i. Was I on the verge of trapping myself like Gilligan and his fellow castaways?

In the pond, a large red and black koi fish swam to us, begging for food. My wife always has some sort of kiddie food in her handbag, so she brought out crackers, which we crumbled and dropped into the water.

"His name is Midnight," Valerie said.

A white koi with a yellow patch on its head, like a regal crown, appeared from the shadowy depths of the pond and shared the snack.

"That one is Princess Di. You can even pet her."

Just then a school of tilapia, dark and about the size of trout, raced across the pond, snapping like piranhas at the crumbs.

Valerie wanted to keep the momentum going. "You haven't seen the best feature yet," she said, walking across the patio. "Watch this." She flipped a switch. I heard a splashing sound and looked to the far side of the pond: a waterfall gushing down a pile of lava rocks.

I affected casualness. "What was the asking price again?"

Even more casually than I had asked, she named a price but added conspiratorially, "I'll bet you can offer less. They want to sell to someone with the aloha spirit."

A silence fell. "Perhaps the owners will take a fancy to you," she said coquettishly. "Think about it, then give me a call."

Getting into the car, we looked across the street at the neighbor's house, a turquoise-colored plantation cottage. A cat was sniffing fishnets that hung from its veranda. A dog charged out into the sunlight and chased the cat, until it was jerked back by a chain anchored to the axle of a rusted car. A large Hawaiian man, sprawled in a hammock strung between two dwarf coconut trees, awoke and waved at the dog as if shooing away a fly. Life in this tranquil place seemed to be nothing more than a long nap, with occasional interruptions.

We left Valerie and drove ten houses down to a cottage we'd rented for the week. In front, there was a tan sand beach, and beyond, the white foam of waves breaking in the blue water. They boomed against the barrier reef, sending spray ten feet into the air. I inhaled the clean sea breeze and the sweet odor of coconuts baking in the sun—intoxicating aromas. There on the rental house veranda, we sipped iced tea.

I looked at my Tahitian wife, Paulette, whom I'd met in Waikīkī twenty years before while we were still in college. Like most islanders, she has two names; her "real" one is Li Moe, which means "Beautiful Flower" in Hakka Chinese. She grew up in the fields of Tahiti like the flower that sprouts from a sugarcane. *What a beautiful flower she is to me,* I thought as I stared at her. *If you can find your sugarcane flower, don't let her go but keep her blossoming year after year.* Her hair hung loosely down her back in jet-black ripples, and a white pikake clung above her ear like the pen of a secretary. Her sloe-eyed face smiled with a happy radiance. She was born for island life.

Our two boys, fifteen-year-old Anthony and eleven-year-old Will James, were just unpacking their bags when I called out, "Let's go for a swim."

Anthony loped with a cocky high school teenager's gait. Skinny young Will wiggled with excitement as we pussyfooted over white coral and across black lava rocks to the beach in front of the architect's house. Tidal pools stirred with sea creatures. Careful not to slip on the rocks, we stepped into the sandy shallows, spit in our masks to prevent them from fogging, slipped the straps over our heads, and eased into the warm water.

In this private aquarium, we saw long fish; short fish; tubular fish; fish as square as boxes or as round as soccer balls; fish shaped like sabers, and others like hatchets; fish striped like zebras, spotted like calico, or checked like plaid. A school of tiny fish glittered and darted as if someone had tossed out a handful of shiny new coins. Parrotfish looked as though they had flopped around on a painter's wet palette. A school of butterfly fish fluttered by like yellow flowers blowing in the wind.

And the *honu*—green sea turtles—that glided past us were so numerous we had a hard time not bumping into them. Although the creatures themselves were harmless, their sharp beaks and small beady eyes frightened the boys at first. Their flippers worked like

placid oars. They seemed eternally serene and dignified, and we swam along with them for a time, lost in our lazy float through the coral heads and their millions of years of creation.

A double-hulled wooden canoe with red sails full of breeze soon appeared in the deep blue ocean, a replica of an ancient Polynesian sailing vessel. The dream of transplanting ourselves here was about to become real.

I was reading a book at the time, *Born in Paradise* by Armine von Tempski, who had grown up on neighboring Maui. Encouraged by Jack and Charmian London to write about the beauty of this archipelago, she mused, "Attaining Paradise in the hereafter does not concern me greatly. I was born in Paradise."

CHAPTER TWO

Da Kine House

An island attracts one strangely and inexplicably. . . . And
as we grow older the fascination is not lost. Any man with a
spark of poetry in his soul will stand on the deck of a ship to
stare, captivated, at an island, while a mainland, even though
it be more beautiful, will command but a passing glance.
—ROBERT DEAN FRISBIE, *MY TAHITI*, 1937

The whole family hopped in the car and headed up the road by
the seashore through an oasis of palm, mango, milo, plumeria, and
banana trees to view another property. As we wound inland, the
landscape turned as desolate and arid as the Serengeti plains. Wild
goats poked their horned heads above the black lava rocks and yellow
grass as we turned left onto the Queen Kaʻahumanu[2] Highway. The
boys laughed at the first yellow and black sign that appeared along
the side of the road: "CAUTION Donkeys Crossing." The beasts

---

2. *Pronounced "Kah-ah-who-mah-new." (The vowels are pronounced softly and*
reverently.) Here, even the highways have phonetically beautiful names.

of burden were brought to this remote island to carry its rich coffee beans down from the Kona hills. In the late 1940s, surplus army jeeps were utilized instead; the animals were set free and now ran wild. I, too, wanted to be set free from feeling like a sort of electromagnetic donkey, wired with Wi-Fi, cell phones, and, most of all, other people's endless magnetic resonance and trivia.

Over the radio, an old Hawaiian song played. "I am Havai'i, I am forever... I am Havai'i, I am the flowers." (In the Hawaiian language, *w* is sometimes pronounced as *v*.) The deejay followed with "Aloha, dis is Kahikina, here on another terrible Tuesday, to tell you 'bout tings I nevah know." After spouting some trivia, he added, "If you

at work, no sleep, eh? Just stare at your computah or whatever you doing and just *look* busy. Before you know it, *pau hana* time, den go home and relax wit your favorite kine beverage, and den what's fo' *kaukau*, maybe a little laulau? Too tired? Make rice and beans and open a can of Spam. Mo' bettah, come on down for da kine *ono* sushi at Wasabe's! In downtown Kailua-Kona, Hawai'i, USA." Then the long drawn-out jingle: *"Wah—sah—bay's!"*

Before our eyes passed the loveliest vista I'd ever seen in all my island travels: the top of Mauna Kea was covered in snow; yet on that December day, we were wearing sandals and shorts. To the south, Mauna Loa's white cap glistened against the blue sky. Already the sun was so bright that it would make the colors too milky for photos, so I kept driving as the radio sounded on.

"And now, folks, here's a little music to soothe da savage driver." A beautiful male voice began singing in falsetto to a gentle Hawaiian melody, "Kiss and Never Tell."

"I used to sing like that when I was about nine years old. Now I sing like a *man*," Kahikina said once the song had faded out, his voice going basso profundo on "man." He then spun a few Jawaiian numbers (modern Hawaiian with a reggae beat). Some were songs popular elsewhere but played here with a distinct Hawaiian intonation, usually with ukulele and guitar rhythms. Some were in the Hawaiian language, some were in English, and others were a mixture of English and Hawaiian. Some lamented times gone by, such as this one: "They took the land, they took aloha, they took the queen even though they didn't know her . . . but they couldn't take the *mana*." *Mana* means "spirit," about which we would learn more later.

Fifteen miles farther, at an altitude of three thousand feet, we found ourselves in the cowboy town of Waimea, surrounded by the Parker Ranch—225,000 acres of grazing cattle—and visited several houses in the more gentrified areas of town. One was a large turnkey place with a view of the ocean and the Mauna Kea volcano. A small creek ran through its back garden, and the surrounding brown hills reminded me of the drive from Boise to Sun Valley, Idaho. Logically, this house was the smarter choice: no repairs *and* more affordable.

But that funny beat-up house by the pond was tempting me to take it on, to catch my piece of paradise through its ramshackle doors. I envisioned the bramble-covered backyard becoming a tropical farm lush with lemon, papaya, and mango. Still, I needed some kind of validation. I called Valerie the next day and asked her which one of the houses she thought was the better value. She said the pond house fit us. "It's da kine," she said.

That seemed to sum it all up. In Hawaiian Pidgin English, *da kine* means the kind of thing you were talking or thinking about. Whenever someone says "da kine," the other person is just supposed to *know* what he or she is referring to.

Although the place was a mess, it was da kine and in da kine spot. It was us. We were for it and with it. Even as we had waited years to find such a home this long-unsold house had been waiting for us.

If only we had known what lay ahead.

The remainder of my share of the proceeds from the sale of our old family ranch in Napa Valley would be just enough for the down payment on the Hawaiian shack/studio and the house on stilts over the pond. Dispossessed of land, I longed to have some dirt under my feet, but my wish was an old sailor's dream—a salty piece of earth a stone's throw from the ocean. Besides, while Hawai'i is famed for shark attacks and pesky insects, it is home to no snakes. I wasn't nostalgic for the rattlesnakes coiled in the grass near my family's Napa barn.

The media say the Aloha State is undergoing a modern land rush led by tech billionaires, greedy developers, reclusive actors and musicians, deep-sea fishermen, golf nuts, survivalists, and people burned out on urban life. Waikīkī Beach on the island of Oʻahu has indeed begun to resemble Miami Beach. Yet in Kohala, on the northwest coast of the Big Island, little has changed, and that suited us just fine.

Valerie invited us for drinks and hors d'oeuvres at her place so we could meet the owner of the house. Bill, a dignified eighty-five-year-old retired architect, had designed many of the houses in the area since the early 1970s. He told us how he loved Hawaiʻi and had many ideas for shaping up the house. "But," he said quite simply, "I'm just too old."

Paulette and I wanted that place, just as once—twenty years ago—we had wanted each other. The symptoms were similar: delirious desire one minute and, the next, a sinking into doubt that our passionate ambitions would ever be fulfilled. And so, the following day, we met up for lunch with Valerie at a café in Waimea.

We ordered the Waipiʻo Ways: fresh ahi tuna, ono (also known as wahoo), local sweet potatoes, and taro and sweet Maui onions on a bed of Waimea lettuce—Hawaiian health food, *onolicious*.[3]

Over mango ice cream, we made an offer that might satisfy the bank liens and the owner. "I don't think you'll regret it," said Valerie. "I'll get the papers ready."

Paulette and I celebrated our decision that evening over dinner at a nearby seashore resort, where a guitarist sang classic Hawaiian songs in a deep voice.

The music melded with its setting so perfectly that the island itself seemed to be calling to us. "Dreams come true in blue Havaiʻi," sang

---

3. A *"Hawenglish"* word. Ono means *"good"* in Hawaiian.

the musician, and it seemed so. There we sat at our table, Paulette and I. Our two *hapa* boys, sporting flower-print aloha shirts,[4] read their menus in a well-mannered way, reminding me of my own childhood.

Born in San Francisco, I first voyaged to the islands by Matson liner in 1959 as a three-year-old. Then Tahiti, two summers in a row. In the summer of 1967, our family rented a house past Diamond Head on O'ahu. My brother, sister, and I took surfing lessons at Waikīkī Beach and learned how to play the ukelele. Now the resort guitarist belted out the songs I had learned more than thirty years before, including "My Little Grass Shack in Kealakekua, Hawaii," the lyrics of which now struck me as fateful. Paulette's glance told me she'd picked up on it too.

With imagination, we can visualize the routes of our lives forking and then joining together. In the late seventies, I worked a season as a room-service waiter in a hotel on Maui and studied business in Honolulu. Later, after a stint as a stills photographer, I landed a job as production assistant for Dino De Laurentiis on a series of films, including the Mel Gibson version of *The Bounty*, which was filmed in Dino's favorite spot—the islands of Tahiti. There, I shot magazine photos, sailing to many South Sea isles on the decks of tramp steamers and living in real grass shacks.

I clerked in Paulette's family's general store for a time, then, after years in Polynesia, I returned to the mainland with my bride to resume a conventional life. Now, fifteen years later, here we were on this restaurant veranda, breathing sensuous ocean air laced with garden perfume. The music and wine stimulated in me a mix of nostalgia and a longing to start a new island-style life. As I looked

---

4. *The colorful patterned aloha shirts are considered formal or business attire in Hawai'i.*

at my family, emotions overwhelmed me; I excused myself for a moment alone and walked down to the small beach.

A manta ray was gliding through the water toward a light. The waves smacked the shore, and it hit me that I was back on the Polynesian islands that had long ago stolen my young heart and had now lured me to return with my wife and children. Was it possible to attain the dreams of a long-faded youth?

We went back to the mainland, with hopes of returning with the keys to the house.

CHAPTER THREE

Night of the Insects

*Oh, fill me up about this lovely country! You can go on writing
that slop about balmy breezes and fragrant flowers, and all that
sort of truck, but you're not going to leave out them santipedes . . .*
—MARK TWAIN, LETTERS FROM HAWAII, 1866

A month later, I paused at the top of the aircraft stairs and inhaled
the air of Hawai'i—a distinctly tropical perfume of humidity, rot-
ting coconuts, sea salt, and volcanic ash. The adventure had begun.
Camping in our new house, we cooked our meals in a pot and a pan
that we'd carried in our suitcases, and we served them on cardboard
boxes. On the third night, the breeze gave way to muggy stillness.
"Bug night" began with the appearance of a few insects followed
by sprinting geckos lashing their tongues. Then a profusion of bugs
covered the walls. Armies of carpenter ants filed in from small cracks
everywhere in the house. Three-inch-long cockroaches scurried; we
swatted them with our slippers. It was like a science fiction movie.

A bug scream is different from any other kind. It usually comes out something like "Yeechs uh uh ahhhh!" in a high-pitched whine of fear and loathing. One evening at sunset, I walked head-on into a spiderweb on the upstairs balcony. All I saw were orange and black legs, striped like a tiger's, and the torso of a large cane spider dangling off my forehead. After I did a sped-up Samoan slap dance, it dropped to the floor and scampered away.

We slept on inflatable mattresses atop the old carpet while mosquitoes attacked us with relentless rapacity. We could feel bugs crawling on us. Mainly, they were just the harmless carpenter ants; but I feared the infamous centipede, whose sting is stronger than that of a dozen wasps. Centipedes in the islands are equipped with two large pincers for injecting venom into their prey, and their legs scratch with venom as well. Their backs are hard, and if you manage to chop one in half, then you have two wiggling menaces to deal with.

Will was afraid, although there were few bugs in his downstairs room; they seemed to congregate in the living room and the stairway and in our bedroom. Quite reasonably, he yearned for real furniture. Paulette commented, "I'm glad we only have boys."

The next day, we went down to the Tropical Sleep Center in Kailua. The owner, "Doc," offered to deliver a fine bed the following day. "My pleasure." There is something to be said for the small independent businesses of America, whose owners make the extra personal effort.

We told Doc about the bugs. He asked if we had seen little black spiders.

"You mean those cute little ones that hop and jump?" I said.

"Yeah, those da buggahs. Smash 'em or they'll crawl in your bed at night—itching welts. A nuisance."

Doc tilted his glasses down, looked at me, and said, "Have you heard of the new brown spider?"

I told him I hadn't.

"So toxic, it rots your skin. A chunk of your flesh has to be surgically removed," Doc said, while slicing the air with his hand. "Good news: only over in Hilo, where they escaped from a container full of plants from Asia. Needs a wet climate."

We returned to our house that evening with a can of bug spray and put a dent in the insect population, but while I was in a deep sleep, something bit me. It was a torturous, nasty awakening, as if I'd been stabbed with a penknife. I sat up, clutched my stinging inner left thigh, and let out a painful scream. My flashlight revealed a large centipede wiggling toward the closet on more than a hundred legs. I grabbed a shoe, but it slithered into a tiny crack in the wall.

Down in the kitchen, I put lemon on the welt. There were two bleeding holes like a rattlesnake bite almost at my testicles. I had heard that some Polynesians place a lighted cigarette close to the bitten area so that the immediate heat relieves the sting. I lit up a Cohiba cigarillo and put the fire-hot tip near the red holes on the swelling bump. A warm tea bag also gave some relief, then ice, and, finally, a cold beer inside *and* out.

In the Marquesas Islands, shortly before his arrival in Hawai'i, Herman Melville was bitten by something on the leg; it became infected, causing fevers and temporary lameness. In *Typee*[5] he wrote that a "congenial inhabitant of the chasm" had bitten him. It was most likely a centipede.

---

5. *The novel was based on Melville's experience of deserting his whaling ship and seeking refuge in the dreaded cannibal valley of Taipi on Nuku Hiva. After the Marquesas and Tahiti, Melville left the whaling service in 1843 to spend three months working for a merchant in Honolulu. He made himself unpopular among the American residents and missionaries there by favoring a British occupation. When he tired of the arrogance of the Europeans and what he saw as the degeneracy of the Hawaiians, he shipped back to Boston.*

Mark Twain crawled into bed one night in Hawai'i, and a centipede bit him. After that, he always checked between the sheets first. Twain wrote in his *Letters from Hawaii* about a certain Captain Godfrey who got off easy, "because he always carried a bottle full of scorpions and santipedes soaked in alcohol, and whenever he got bit, he bathed the place with that devilish mixture or took a drink out of it, I don't recollect which."

In the tropics, bugs are a fact of life.

A couple of days later, three burly Hawaiians showed up early in the morning and tacked down new carpet. Just as they left, a truck pulled up and delivered our bamboo couch, coffee table, chairs, side table, and colorful pillows, giving our beach shack a cozy feeling. A real home.

Luana, the insurance lady, arrived the following morning. "Aloha. Thought I'd get here early—pictures for our files." Although she looked pure Hawaiian, she volunteered, "I'm part Hawaiian, part

Japanese, part Irish, and, oh, I forgot one." She looked up at the sky and thought for a moment, then lapsed easily into Pidgin. "Oh yah, Portuguee, my grandmudah, my auntie too. Befo' she hav' one *hale* here. We wen' go here summah time. Dees ponds, da bee ponds, cause all da kine bees."

As if on cue, a couple of large black bumblebees flew past us and landed on some beautiful orange flowers. "Des flowers, from da kou tree, like Puako, where dis place got its name, yah," she said. She pronounced it "Pooh-ah-ko," accent on "ko," not "Pooh-whacko," the way most newcomers mangle the pronunciation.

I pointed to a few sugarcane stalks next to the kou tree and told her, "I read somewhere that Puako means 'the stem and the tassel of the sugarcane.'"

"Oh, yeah, dat too, just spell different, yah." She shrugged. "*Pua* means 'flower.'"

One of my goals was to learn as many Hawaiian words as I could, but I was having a hard time with the vowel pronunciation. Nevertheless, I plunged right in with what I thought would be a compliment: "You smell like a pooh-ah-ah."

Luana laughed so hard, she might have wet her pants. Yes, we white mainlanders sure are fun to laugh at.

"*Pooh-ah* means flower," she said. "But *puaʻa* means . . ." Between giggles and gulps of air, she spurted out, "*Puaʻa* means . . ." Laughing uncontrollably again, she held her arms around her stomach and slapped her hip, as if it might help her to stop. Once she regained her composure, she said, "You say I smell like *pig*."

The language would humble me more than once.

"Ah, dunno." She held up her arms, with her palms facing the sky like a hula dancer's, and said, "According to ancient legend and our *kupuna*—you know, our elders—dis place actually name afta Princess Puako."

"A real princess?" I asked.

"Da kine," she said. "Dey say she from Puna, odda side, yah." She pointed southeast toward Mauna Loa. She explained that the princess walked across the lava fields in search of *he'e*, octopus, "her favorite kine food." And when she reached the beach, she met Ne'ula, a woman who introduced her to her son, Lalamilo, who was a fisherman. "He da guy, yah. He compared Puako to finest *he'e* he ever catch, den, love at first sight. Dey marry, he catch plenny *tako*, den she fat as whale, and dey call da place Puako, yah."

Luana climbed down to the lava rocks by the edge of the pond. After fiddling with her digital camera, she photographed the cottage. Just then, the renters—Susanna, the cocktail waitress, and her henpecked husband, the diving instructor—came out onto the deck over the pond. Awakened from sleep, they didn't smile, even after the good-natured Luana waved. They walked out the gate in a huff, hopped in their Jeep, and spewed gravel all over the driveway in a display of territorial defiance.

"Got rentahs?" Luana said, in more of a statement than a question. She scribbled something on a pad.

"We gave them notice because we needed to remodel, and they accused us of evicting them."

"You beddah off. Too much preshah, pain in da *okole*. Whatsa fo' matta wit dem? Give us stink eye, yah," Luana said. She glanced at the Mickey Mouse watch on her wrist. "*Auwe*, gotta go. No dress up like dis all da time." She glanced down at her black matching skirt and top, lifted her right leg back, and stared at the mud caking the bottom of her high-heeled shoes. "*Pilau* pond."

She turned to me. "Hilo, funeral. My auntie, she die. Da kine have summah house, down der." She pointed down the road and said sadly, "Ah, summahs, so wonderful back den, just play on da beach, fish by da reef, dance hula, sing meles, and chew on sugarcane. Jus sing and laugh, dos da kine days."

Luana quickly shrugged off her musing, and her normal, carefree countenance returned. "Aloha," she said and smiled. She waved goodbye with a flick of her wrist as elegant as a hula dancer's moving hands.

I thought, *What a wonderful place where saying hello and goodbye is "Love"—not "How are you doing?" or "So long," but "Love."*

"Aloha," I replied. Then, "Mahalo." No *malihini*, I.

Paulette asked me what the insurance lady and I had been talking about for so long. "Oh, just flowers, pigs, and love."

"Love?" she said, frowning.

"Yeah, you know *ah-low-ha*, da kine love, the aloha spirit. Remember, we're in Hawai'i."

CHAPTER FOUR

Bushwhacking

The sun smote us fair and full; the air streamed from the hot rock, the distant landscape gleamed and trembled through its vortices.
—ROBERT LOUIS STEVENSON, _TRAVELS IN HAWAII_, 1889

Flora flourish in volcanic soil, and the jungle had taken over our backyard; it needed to be cleared.

A large Hawaiian guy pulled up in a flatbed truck and sauntered into the yard. His brown belly spilled out of a tank top and hung over his dirty blue jeans. We shook hands and he said, "Gus Rawson."

Gus and I walked the property as he made a bid to clear the land. He was articulate, and without a hint of an islander's accent.

"I'm not from Hawai'i," he eventually volunteered. "Montana."

"You could have fooled me."

He explained that his mother was Hawaiian and his father was from Helena. As a kid he'd occasionally visited relatives in Hawai'i, but in his twenties he'd moved over for good. "Tired of shoveling snow," he said.

A tattoo of a Native American woman was inked into his right bicep. She resembled Sacagawea, the Shoshone woman who guided Lewis and Clark, or at least, as I remembered her from the bronze statue in Fort Benton, Montana, where my great-grandfather settled in 1870. After I told him that my grandparents were also from Helena, then moved to San Francisco, Gus said, "Big Island, small world!"

I gave him a deposit. A couple of days later, while I was sipping my first cup of coffee at about 7:00 a.m., an older Caucasian man in overalls and what looked like a train conductor's hat appeared on the back porch. "Gus sent me. I thought I'd get an early start. Homer's my name," he mumbled through his few remaining teeth.

A few minutes later a couple of twenty-year-old Hawaiians showed up with chain saws and cans of gasoline. Homer explained, "The boys'll buck up all these logs into more manageable pieces until we can get Bessie in through the back."

"Bessie?"

"That's the tractor's name. Gus does good on backhoe. But he don't know jack shit about septics. Yes sirree! Yesterday he ran right over a tank a couple of lots down. Shit all over the place. Yes sirree. Don't worry, I've been doing this for a couple of years. Before, I was in the military. Based in Wah-e-wah, Oh-wa-who."

"How long were you in the service?" I asked.

"Twenty-seven years, five months, seventeen days, eight hours, and fifteen minutes, yes sirree!" he said.

Somehow Homer reminded me of Jim Nabors,[6] who always said, "Golly, Sarge" in the sitcom *Gomer Pyle U.S.M.C.*

---

6. *Nabors, a resident of the islands, had for years performed in "A Merry Christmas with Friends and Nabors." Local singers, hula dancers, and the Honolulu Symphony made it a show found only in Hawai'i.*

I asked Homer what he did in the military. He replied, "Mechanic, yes sirree! Retired, and moved to Hah-why-yah."

All morning, the terrifying sound of trees crashing came from the jungle behind our house. The diesel engine *chug, chug, chugged*, and Bessie's tracks clanked across the lava rocks. Gus was at the controls, bouncing and pitching in the rough terrain like he was riding a mule. While he cleared the land, the bronzed young men, Keoni and Rocky, ever cool in their wraparound sunglasses, kept the chain saws buzzing, chopping up the large fallen tree trunks. "As soon as we hit that big pile over there," said Gus, "we're going to see all kinds of bugs and rats come flyin' outta there."

I offered ten dollars to the young men for any rat killed. We waited with shovels in hand until Gus hit the pile with the tractor. Like a dream of the Pied Piper, rats came scampering out of the brush. I whacked one with the shovel—beginner's luck. With our boots we squished a few centipedes the size of hotdogs; they wriggled but still repeatedly struck the leather of our boots with their venomous pincers. *Revenge.* I hit a few of those vile serpentine creatures with a shovel. Even three weeks after being bitten, my thigh was still sore and bore two scars.

While sipping coffee the next morning on the back porch, I looked out at the brush in the backyard and saw Keoni poke a stick at a half-dead rat. "Got one," he said and smiled proudly. I handed him a ten-dollar bill.

The following morning, two Micronesians stood in the backyard. "Where are Keoni and Rocky?" I asked.

"Surf's up!" said the tall, wiry one, who introduced himself as Buni.

"Dose guys no work when dere's surf," said the other man, short and muscular. "Me Buhtani."

I asked them where they were from, and they said, "Bikini Atoll," in the Marshall Islands. Someone mentioned nuclear bomb tests. Buni knocked Buhtani's hat off to reveal a bald spot. We all laughed.

"I lived in the Society Islands for many years," I said. I took off my hat and pointed to my own bald spot. "Mururoa, French bomb tests."

They laughed harder. Their good natures and humor had helped them survive the displacement of relocation after the American tests left Bikini laced with dangerous levels of radioactivity. Many Micronesians had moved to Hawai'i. Others were moved to smaller atolls in the Marshalls, where they gave up their traditional life, living in shanties and eating food out of tin cans. (Incidentally, four days after the United States detonated nuclear bombs on Bikini, *le bikini*, a tiny two-piece bathing suit named after the atoll was invented in the South of France.)

Whoever said islanders are lazy? Over the next few days, the landscapers hauled and cleared fallen coconut trees and kiawe branches at a rapid pace. Buni kept a steady supply of green coconuts open for drinking. The water tastes surprisingly similar to the soft drink Sprite, only without the sugar, and it is so clean it can be used for sterilization. One day Buni split open a heart of palm. The velvety, tender white flesh, delicious and refreshing, had just a slight taste of coconut.

Wearing boots and gloves, I hauled brush for hours until exhausted—great stress therapy. Then the tractor hit a large pile of logs. What appeared to be smoke enveloped Gus, and he shouted and slapped his body, jumping up from the driver's seat as if a swarm of wasps were attacking him.

I ran over. "Are you okay?" I asked.

"Oh, that's hot!" Gus shouted. "Yeah, I'm fine. Just steam. Radiator pipe broke. Darn."

Homer assessed the damage. "Gotta go to Hilo and get a new radiator thingamajig," he said.

"Yes sirree," I said, finishing his statement.

Mana means authority, spiritual power, or spirit essence in a person, place, or object. In ancient Polynesian culture, *mana* was believed to be a supernatural or divine endowment. In Western terms it can be described as the radiance of one's soul. In today's urban terms, *mana* can be like the "up" feeling of having a shine on your shoes and a melody in your heart, when the whole world is turning your way and you're on top of it.

I believed this house and property had a lot of *mana*. But it was in dire need of a makeover. I was over forty, and I wasn't getting any younger. Or was I? Helping out with the work, I was sweating off pounds, building muscles, and even sleeping better. The place was sharing its *mana*. We had come to Hawai'i for restoration—not just of the house and our land but also ourselves.

In late June we enrolled our two boys in a summer school in the foothills of Mauna Kea. At our house, the logs and brush were neatly cleared, but the flat English lawn I'd envisioned was still a wavy, muddy expanse of dips and bumps—a far cry from cricket-pitch smoothness. Patches of green sprouted here and there, but high winds constantly blew in volcanic dirt from across the lava fields. A layer of black dust covered the house and ended up everywhere, including in our ears. Nevertheless, landscaping and dirt were the least of our worries.

A shiny new pickup truck arrived in our driveway. "Power Construction" was painted on its front doors, over a picture of a baseball player swinging a gigantic hammer like a bat, and the slogan "With Power You're on the Ball!"

The door opened and out stepped Bob Power, a contractor we had booked for the summer. His forearms bulged like Popeye's as his rough hand crushed mine. There was a peculiar protuberance from his lower lip, and he spat, discharging a wad of chewing tobacco onto the ground.

"This here's my partner, Harry," Bob said. "Harry and I built houses together in Vegas. Going way back. Countless tract homes and deluxe houses."

Harry's lanky arms were covered with layers of black hair. Although his cheeks were clean-shaven, he had a thick mustache and a long wavy mane. Hair seemed to come out of everywhere—his ears and nose and along the nape of his neck. As profusely as grass grows on a golf course, hair sprouted from the top of his T-shirt and under his arm sleeves. Harry was as hairy as a man could be.

Bob and Harry unloaded the truck. Soon an air compressor was coughing, humming, and hissing, saws were screeching and whining, and hammers were pounding and smacking. Harry wielded a sledgehammer like a baseball player at batting practice, true to the truck's logo. "I just love demo!" he growled with a maniacal grin as he knocked out the closets in the studio.

Inspired by his gusto for destruction, I picked up a large hammer and took a few whacks at my newly acquired house. The cracking, splintering sound was strangely pleasurable. "I just can't let you have all the fun," I said and began vigorously attacking the walls.

With the aid of a crowbar, progress went well. It felt satisfying, but after an hour I was dripping in sweat and took a breather. "So, Harry," I said, "what's with the logo of the baseball player on Bob's truck?"

"Oh, that," said Harry. "Bob used to play ball, shortstop, for a season, then was cut." Then with a wistful, faraway look in his eyes, he said, "I also played ball. The Houston Nighthawks, Minors, third base for a spell."

"Wow, pro ball. What happened?" I asked.

"Threw my elbow out, then they threw me out. Pissed away all the money. Now I'm just pounding nails."

I asked Harry what he liked best about the pro circuit. Without hesitation he said, "Mazatlán, my early days in the Winter League. Mexicans love baseball. But I like it here too. Hot. And every day it's like mañana, man, laid-back. Hawai'i's just like Mexico, except they speak English!" Then he broke out in a maniacal hack.

"Weather here's the same, kind of sticks," he said. "Joke, huh—sticky weather."

"It's *not* sticky," said Bob in a gravelly voice as he entered the studio. "Dry as a desert. Back to work, eh? Time is money and we're on the clock."

In the afternoon the dust blew in from the lava fields. With a hammer in his hand, Harry commented, "Dirt, dirt everywhere, even in our hair."

Harry seemed to be a few pineapples short of a bushel, but he came up with amusing comments. After a particularly strong gust of wind ripped through the studio, he observed that it was "Blowing harder than a whore on a Saturday night at a Rotary Club meeting." *Bad-a-bing.*

He and Bob also tacked tin bands to the coconut trees to keep the rats from climbing up to their favorite food source. By five o'clock both men looked pretty beat. While Bob put away all the tools, Harry swept out the studio and made sure everything was neat and tidy. I noticed that they worked well together and in sync, each instinctively knowing the other's moves, as if they had been on the same team for a long time.

"See ya tomorrow, same time," said Bob, starting the old truck. Harry waved from the passenger window. As they ambled down the road, Bob stuck his head out and spat a sluice of tobacco on the hot pavement.

Though the tin bands helped, rats ruled. Bob and Harry cut and removed a large panel off the side of the house and found no sign of rodents. "They're in here somewhere," said Harry. "Come on out, you rat-faced crappers." We opened up another panel. Still no luck. Soon we were tearing apart the nice new house.

Harry stood on a ladder and said, "Demo the whole house! We'll find them rats." He laughed his maniacal hack.

Bob stared at him hard and he shut up. Harry sighed, repeating Bob's usually barked mantra, "Back to work."

The abundance of fruit trees in the garden created a rats' paradise. And our resentful renters from the cottage had been stashing their garbage cans near the larger house—a rats' diner. It kept potential buyers at bay so they could stay as long as possible. Rats scampered nightly around the pond; I even saw them taking moonlit swims across it.

When not eating, rats have sex—sometimes twenty times per day. An average litter consists of eight to ten young rats, and the gestation period is twenty-one days. Sexually mature in three months, a grown female may have as many as eight hundred grandchildren. That's why mongooses were imported to Hawai'i. However, the fact that rats are nocturnal and mongooses are diurnal was overlooked.

I'd bought a Hawaiian sling for fishing but hadn't had a chance to use it. The long spear, with a forked end and an elastic rubber sling near the handle, remained in a corner of my studio. One evening I heard a rat in the closet. That did it. I grabbed the spear, drew back the sling, and opened the closet door. There sat a fat, feisty rat, over a foot long including its tail. I let the spear fly. As the fork tips grazed its flank, the rat cried, "Sweeeee!" It stopped to hiss at me before scampering into a hole in the wall.

At the hardware store, I bought half a dozen electric rat zappers. Over the next two weeks, we sent more rodential inmates to the electric chair than a Texas jury; the machines wore out and broke.

Besides carrying mites and viruses, rats bring microbes from sewage, spreading trichinosis, tularemia, and leptospirosis. They have been responsible for the deaths of ten million people in the last century, and during the Middle Ages, the lice-borne plague—the Black Death—killed a third of all Europeans.

War. Bob and I spread out a set of the architect's blueprints on the living room floor and pored over them like military strategists. The rats, we deduced, were getting into the overhang above the porch and the front door. "Then they slide their rats' asses into the walls," said Bob, "and pop out in the stairs." Over the next few hours, Bob and Harry set up an elaborate scaffolding system outside, near the front entryway. After their lunch break, they roved the entire roof of the entry porch.

"Awesome! Pay dirt," said Bob from the top of the scaffold.

"What is it?" I asked.

"Rat shit," he replied.

With an industrial vacuum cleaner, he sucked out the vile waste. "Man, it's already full," he said. "Have to dump it and come back tomorrow."

The next morning, Bob proudly said, "We got over twenty pounds of crap."

For a few days, I climbed up the scaffold and poured gallons of Pine-Sol and Odor-Off into the entry overhang. Once it had aired out, Bob and Harry plugged up all the holes with foam and steel wool and put the roof back on.

Then Bob's industrial vacuum cleaner clogged. "Rats," he brooded. But I had a plan. I would use my new home-improvement purchase, the electric pressure hose, "guaranteed to pressure-wash everything: boats, cars, patios!" I thought it was a no-brainer—do just like the guy in the television ad, turn on the pressure hose, and blast the shit out of the shit.

Luckily for me, we had hired a cleaning person, starting that day. Talihua was one of the oddest people to set foot on our property. Nevertheless, he was kind and a terrific worker. He roared up the driveway on a Harley chopper and took off his helmet. A small black ponytail flopped out and fell down his back. A mixture of Filipino, Hawaiian, and Indonesian, he was no more than five foot two. His face was as smooth as a girl's, with a bit of blue on the shaved chin. He took off his leather jacket and hung it on the back of the motorcycle. He carried a basket woven from palm leaves to the porch, sat down on the steps, and unlaced his black Doc Martens. "I just need a place to change into my work clothes," Talihua said.

Paulette showed him to the hallway bathroom. He emerged wearing a sarong tied in the feminine way, covering his breasts. He wore slippers and sashayed into the kitchen, where he began cleaning the stove. He was a *mahu*, a man/woman, a *kane/wahine*, or quite simply, a transvestite. Talihua did an excellent job waxing the floors and thoroughly cleaned the entire house like a seasoned professional. Mindful of that timeless saying "It is so hard to get good help these days," we didn't want to scare Talihua away on the first day by asking him to do the rat closet. So we waited a week.

The next time Talihua roared up on his Harley, I showed him the closet. "I'll leave my Doc Martens on," he said quietly. Then he wrapped a bandana around his face like a bank robber. I put on work boots myself and wrapped an old T-shirt around my face. I slipped on plastic gloves and handed a pair to Talihua, then I stepped into the closet with the pressure hose and pulled the trigger—rat shit came out of everywhere and landed all over the place, including on me. As I sprayed, Talihua swept the fecal puddles off the patio. With a shovel, I scooped up a ripe dead rat. As Talihua held open a plastic garbage bag to receive the foul critter, he shrieked, "Oooohhhh!" It was too much for him. He handed me the bag, held his hands in the air, wiggled his fingers, and ran into the garden to vomit.

Talihua returned to the chore, and we cleaned out the entire laundry room, ending the day covered in rat droppings from hat to boots. The fetid smell was nauseating. Talihua, usually easygoing, twitched and twittered, then became bitchy. I noticed that he hadn't shaved that morning and was scratching a scraggly growth of angry chin whiskers. I paid Talihua a bonus for cleaning far beyond the call of janitorial duty, and this appeared to restore his morale. Hips swaying, he walked to his Harley, mounted it, and sped off with straight shoulders, a jolly grin on his face, and renewed *mana*.

One day while Bob and Harry were installing track lights on the vaulted ceiling of the living room, I mentioned that my shoulder had been bothering me for some time. A Hawaiian worker they had brought along for that week stepped down from the ladder and said, "Avoid man in white coat with sharp knife, yah. As the kahuna say, put noni juice on it. Look you have noni plants here." He pointed to a plant sprawling over the entranceway that bore oval green-and-white fruit with diamond-shaped markings.

"On the other hand," he said, "too much trouble peeling and straining the juice, and ooh, that smell." He scrunched up his nose and made a face. "Like Camembert cheese."

"Plenty hippie pick 'em. No work for chiefs. Just go to health food store," he added.

"Thanks for the advice," I said. I had heard of noni; it grows in many parts of the world, including Indonesia, where people use it to relieve the aches and pains of arthritis and other discomforts.

The next day in Waimea, I bought a bottle of noni juice mixed with olive oil. I rubbed a decent handful onto my shoulder and, bingo, the pain went away—for a while at least.

After fifteen years of living on the mainland, I had lost something in the hustle and bustle of the modern world. I needed to get my *mana* back. My physical and mental powers had become worn out and needed rejuvenation.

Every night, I fell asleep to the *hush-hushing* sound of waves lapping against the shore, and the trade winds gently rustling the fronds of the coconut trees towering above our house. In the morning I awoke to birds chirping. After a cup of aromatic Kona coffee, I spent the mornings with builders and ordered materials. About midday I'd stretch out in the shade of a coconut tree on the beach, enjoying the sea breeze. Then I'd jog to the end of the road and head back for a cold outdoor shower, followed by a light lunch. Sometimes it was salad or a piece of ahi or ono. We followed the "Waipi'o Diet," also known as the "Wai'anae Diet." Similar to the ancient Hawaiians' repast, it consisted of vegetables, fruits, yams, fish, and poultry found only on the islands. Paulette would go to the local farmer's market and buy fresh taro, breadfruit, purple sweet potatoes, *liliko'i* (passion fruit), guava, lychees, macadamia nuts, grapefruit, tangerines, apple bananas, and ginger.

In the late afternoon I would drive up to Waimea to pick up the boys from summer school. At its higher altitude, Waimea is pleasantly cool and refreshing, especially if it is raining. I breathed easily there and counted my blessings. I would look out at the immense sea and sky, the absence of industrialization that makes Hawai'i seem like a frontier of the modern world, and think of the islands' oft-said phrase "Lucky you live Hawai'i," which seemed so true.

On weekends, the children, off from summer school, were jubilant to have a beach house on an island. The funkier the surf shack was, the cooler they thought their surroundings were.

Some days I walked across the street to the beach, snorkeled, and explored the tidal pools. On calm days, through a pass in the reef, I'd swim far out to where a ledge drops off into the deep blue ocean—a favorite spot for the dive boats—and into an underwater cave full of fish, lobsters, and octopuses. There were puffer fish, like sea porcupines, and elegant Moorish idols striped yellow and black. A yellow-lined goatfish, called *weke* in Hawaiian, had what looked like whiskers hanging from its chin. And the brightly colored turkey fish, *nohu pinao*, swam dangerously close by with its poisonous spines. A moray eel, *puhi*, popped its hideous head out of a hole with a threatening glance.

My *mana* was coming back.

Working in the garden was another way to catch particles of *mana*. It was the quality of the work, turning something ugly into something pretty, that was fulfilling. I was happily venturing, gaining a new life in Hawai'i.

Will, the young artist of our family, was constantly drawing pictures with little slogans. He drew the outline of an island with palm trees and the prophetic words "It is better to live on an island than in a city." He was becoming an island boy.

Summer came to end. We flew back to work, leaving the contractors alone. *Bad idea.*

CHAPTER FIVE

The Contracting Blues

I wish I could tell you about the sweating jungle, the
full moon rising behind the volcanoes, and the waiting.
The waiting. The timeless, repetitive waiting.

—JAMES MICHENER, *TALES OF THE SOUTH PACIFIC*, 1947

In the middle of a hectic fall schedule in San Francisco, we took a break, returned to the islands, and pulled into the driveway. The rental car's air conditioner didn't function, turning it into a sort of mobile sweat lodge. I unstuck myself from the seat and got out.

Bob was there to greet us and show us the building progress, or lack of it. We entered the studio, and he pointed at the new tri-panel glass doors, which slid back into a recess in the wall.

"Very trick," he said, spitting a wad of chewing tobacco off the deck and into the pond. A tilapia immediately hit it. The open-air view was of the pond, waterfall, palm trees, and the vast expanse of wilderness beyond. We assured him it looked "very trick" indeed. The ʻōhiʻa wood poles gave a real Polynesian feel to the corners of the porch. Sunk into the mud, they looked as strong as the columns of the Parthenon.

"The bifold doors for the entryway should be here next week, and the louvered panel windows are still on back order from Honolulu," Bob said. One delay had followed another. I learned the number-one rule of construction: be there.

The bills for labor and materials had been rising dramatically for some months now. Whole walls had been ripped out due to termite damage, revealing half-finished electrical work, and the site now had a semi-demolished rather than polished look.

One day when Bob and Harry went for a lumber run to town, I ducked into the cottage where we had let Harry stay all fall. I was looking for a bar of soap that I had left under the bathroom sink. When I opened the cabinet doors, I saw several hypodermic needles. Harry had said he was diabetic, but was that all he used the needles for? I had heard that this area of the island had been a haven in the seventies and eighties for drug addicts and marijuana growers.

I got my answer a couple of days later when I came home to find Bob and Harry in a heated argument on the porch over the tidal pond. "If you weren't always on the stuff, we might get the job done," Bob said.

"Right, Bob, blame it all on me. Just like you did when Mom left us in the trailer in Vegas and ran off with the croupier."

"You're a failure, Harry." Bob pointed his finger at him. "A failure. You blew your baseball career." Harry then pushed Bob hard, almost sending him into the pond. But Bob recovered and continued to taunt Harry. "You're a loser, a druggie, Harry."

In a fit of frustration, Harry kicked him twice in the leg. In return, Bob popped him on the nose. Harry held his hands to his face, took a couple of steps back, and fell into the pond. Luckily, it was high tide, and he landed in the mud at the deep end and not on the lava rocks.

No time to say anything, I just stood there with groceries in hand and mouth agape. I put the bags down, went over to the deck, and gave Harry a hand out of the pond.

"I quit!" said Harry.

"Well, that's just fine. You're fired," Bob said.

"Listen, you guys," I said. "It's just the heat. Come on now, shake hands. You're professionals. Real contractors, not hooligans, eh?"

They shook hands reluctantly.

"Call it a day," I said. "Tomorrow . . . back to work," I said, repeating Bob's mantra.

The next day, Bob showed up a little late, and Harry was sadly sipping coffee on the very porch he had fallen off the day before.

I met Bob in the driveway and said, "You didn't tell me you two were brothers."

"Yeah, I guess I left out a few things," Bob said.

"Like the needles?"

Bob nodded.

"Maybe you can patch things up," I said, desperate to get the project rolling again and over with.

"Look, I bail him out of jail, give him a job, medical, dental, and he still screws up. What can I say? Either he goes or I go."

I went back into the cottage, where Harry was packing the last of his belongings into a duffel bag. "I ain't working for no Hitler," he said. A few minutes later, he sped away in his rust-speckled truck.

We never did see Harry again, but according to neighbors, he lived out of his truck on some of the vacant lots in the area for some time after that. (Later, we heard that he nearly died of hepatitis, but recovered and went to AA, then played ball on weekends for a club team.)

In America it seems the weirdos always head west. Most just keep going until they reach the coast, but a few head even farther to the Wild West of Hawai'i, in search of paradise. Many of them bring along a plethora of emotional baggage. Some find the answers to their problems, and some don't.

Bob didn't show up for a few days, and with Harry gone, we doubted he could finish by Christmas, when we planned to move in all our furnishings.

One night a wind blew in through the eaves. Down came leaves, dirt, twigs, bugs, and even small scorpions. I smiled uneasily in my sleep. I dreamed that the backyard was burning. I awoke chuckling—I had dreamed the house was on fire and there was no more mess to deal with.

As much as I loathed the construction process, it just *had* to be completed. Anthony was headed off to boarding school, but we had enrolled our younger son, Will, in a local private school for the second term and had already paid for the entire year. Were we going to be a day late and a dollar short?

Two weeks before Christmas, a thirty-foot container was parked on the street in front of our mainland house, twelve miles outside of San Francisco. "Matson" was written in huge letters on the sides of the metallic shipping crate. All the previous week had been spent with movers, packing the contents of our house into boxes, which filled our living room.

We took the sage advice of Chinese practitioners of feng shui: clean up clutter to make room for growth and prosperity. And I listened to the Dalai Lama's advice: only keep things that are useful or that one finds to have great beauty. We gave carloads of clothes, toys, furniture, et cetera, to charities. The remainder of our life-gatherings was packed in the container, sealed, and hauled off.

After I fulfilled a series of book signings and slide lectures for my publishers and my wife got her year-end bonus from the travel agency where she worked, we handed the keys to the renters—a couple with a young child, starting out just as we had fifteen years earlier. Our suburban house would soon be filled with their furniture and dreams. Sad to leave, we were also elated to be moving to the aloha life. Schlepping our briefcases back and forth to the city, we had spent too many years amid the motoring masses, driving down freeways and across bridges to keep appointments. Perhaps we had now found the right exit ramp—*Hawaiʻi*.

But that evening, just before our flight, Veryn, the painter from Hawaiʻi, called to say that the contractor had been so far behind schedule that the interior was still at the caulking and sanding stage. "There's dust everywhere," Veryn said. "Quite frankly, I cannot for the love of God"—and love God he did, being the son of a minister—"see the Conrad family moving in here right now."

At least that is what I pieced together. With the echo and crackling static of his cell phone, it sounded more like "Dust, dust, everywhere. For the love of God, love of God." Then I made out, "Postpone trip or stay-ay in motel-otel. Till finish-inish."

And so it came to pass that we checked into Uncle Billy's in the center of Kailua-Kona during the Christmas season. The hotel, in a 1950s cement building, was decorated with a retro Polynesian motif, and the thatched-roof bar and restaurant advertised an all-you-can-eat buffet dinner for $8.95. *So this is paradise,* I thought, as I stood in the lobby with my family and our considerable luggage—the final move—*to live in the islands forever?* As I watched a gecko sprint across the reception wall and devour a moth, I thought of Noel Coward's assessment of the Pacific Islands: "Reptilian nausea." I had that exhausted traveler's feeling, like I was at the end of Tobacco Road with no tobacco, or in Tijuana without tequila. Maybe a mai tai would do the trick.

I revived when Anthony, who is happy anywhere there is a television during football season, said, "Chill out, Dad. At least we're in Why-ee and not freezing our friggin' butts off." He had a point there.

"But what about Santa Claus?" said our younger son, Will James. "Does he come to hotels?"

"Santa comes straight from the North Pole to Kona to warm up before traveling the world," I said. (I knew that this was the *last* Christmas he'd believe in the Santa Claus myth that we had promulgated for so many years, including by bribing Anthony not to tell.)

The first evening, we walked across the street to the historic Kona Inn. Built in 1928 by the Inter-Island Steam Navigation Company for its passengers, it became a hub for deep-sea fishermen. In the lobby hangs an impressive array of world-record trophies. A 1,103-pound Pacific blue marlin looming over the entryway was a record in the thirty-pound test line category. On the facing wall, a 203-pound yellowfin tuna holds the women's world record for the twenty-pound test line.

On the veranda we ordered ahi sashimi and watched the canoes and boats in the harbor as the sunset moved from glowing orange, to red, to darkness. A series of antique fans, pulled by long leather straps, stirred the air. Perhaps they were the same fans that had cooled John Wayne when he stayed there in 1954 during the making of *The*

Sea Chase, filmed mostly on a freighter off the Kona coast. The Duke married his third wife, Pilar Pallete, nearby at a sunset ceremony.

I thought of Hunter S. Thompson, who would "hunker down in the afternoon at the far end of the Kona Inn bar to read the newspapers and drink cold margaritas," while doing research for *The Curse of Lono*. He wrote, "From my perch at the end of the bar, with the big wooden fans whirling slowly above my head, I could look out on the whole waterfront. It was a good place to relax and read the papers—with the hula class practicing on the lawn, tall coconut palms along the seawall, big sailboats out in the bay and a whole zoo of human weirdness churning quietly all around me."

The following morning we walked down the Kailua waterfront to the Hulihe'e Palace, a columned Victorian building with a large veranda. Inside we found fine furniture made of koa, a beautiful wood from the Hawaiian forests, along with possessions of King Kalakaua and his wife Queen Kapi'olani. In one room was a large koa trunk from 1887, once used for all the queen's fine clothes when she, along with heiress-apparent Princess Lili'uokalani, traveled to England to attend the jubilee celebration of Queen Victoria's fiftieth anniversary of her accession to the throne.

Robert Louis Stevenson spent much time with the king in Honolulu as the two were great friends, as well as at the Hulihe'e

Palace in Kona. Stevenson once described Kalakaua as "a very fine intelligent fellow, but . . . what a crop for the drink!"[7]

In one of the upstairs rooms of the palace, on one of the koa tables, sits a teak and rosewood music box, a gift from RLS to Princess Victoria Ka'iulani, the king and queen's niece and heiress to the throne. Beside it is a copy of a poem Stevenson wrote in 1889, before the half-Scottish princess left for Europe to finish her education.

Forth from her land to mine she goes,
The island maid, the island rose,
Light of heart and bright of face:
The daughter of a double race.

Her islands here, in Southern sun,
Shall mourn their Kaiulani gone,
And I, in her dear banyan shade,
Look vainly for my little maid.

Sadly, the intellectual and bespectacled princess never took the throne. The monarchy was overthrown in 1893 under the leadership of Queen Lili'uokalani, who replaced her brother Kalakaua in 1891 as the ruler of the islands. (On a trip to Mexico and California, Kalakaua suffered a stroke in Santa Barbara and died in the Palace Hotel in San Francisco at the age of fifty-four. His body was shipped back to Honolulu for the royal burial.) Kalakaua's dream of a Pan-Pacific federation was smashed as the United States annexed the Hawaiian Islands in 1898, at the height of the Spanish–American

---

7. *The slim author of* The Strange Case of Dr. Jekyll and Mr. Hyde *apparently wasn't considering Kalakaua's sheer size—twice that of Stevenson's—when marveling at his alcohol consumption.*

War. It was a tumultuous and complicated time in Hawaiian history; there are hundreds of fascinating books written on the subject. The best story may have been written by Liliʻuokalani herself—*Hawaiʻi's Story by Hawaiʻi's Queen*, an eloquent testament to her country. Historian Glen Grant wrote an introduction to a 1990 printing of *Hawaiʻi's Story*: "The struggle of Hawaiian sovereignty has not been dismissed as impractical or impossible, and many native Hawaiians today are aware that the tragic events of 1893 demand a truthful and rigorous reassessment."

After her return from Europe, Kaʻiulani struggled constantly with rheumatism. She went riding in the rain with her friends, the Parker girls, on their colossal ranch, which spreads across the sloping foothills of Mauna Kea, twenty miles from our house in Puako, and caught pneumonia. Her health took a turn for the worse. Kaʻiulani's death in 1899, at the age of twenty-three, marked the end of an era in Hawaiʻi. There is something poignant about this bookworm of a girl dying surrounded by followers. My wife, having grown up in Tahiti, and a good student in the French parochial schools, is particularly moved by the story.

Paulette, the boys, and I left the palace and strolled across the street to the island's oldest Christian church, authorized by King Kamehameha II in 1820. For Asa Thurston, one of the first missionaries at the Moku‘aikaua Church, life away from England was no paradise. According to one of the clippings pinned on a wall in the rear of the church, he described Kailua in 1820 as "A filthy village of thatched huts, built upon beds of indurated lava, on which the fervent sun poured his furnace heat every day in every year." With the help of the Hawaiian people, Thurston designed and built the Moku‘aikaua stone church in 1837. When the cool ocean breeze comes in from the west, it literally flows through the entire length of the building.

Fortunately for us, the island weather is the coolest during the winter months, and on that December morning as we strolled along the sidewalk through town, the waves from Kailua Bay smashed against the break wall with such force that a refreshing spray flew over our heads. Impatiently, I wished aloud that our house would soon be done.

"Chill out, Dad," said Anthony again. "At least we're in Why-ee. Hey, check out this awesome ad." He showed me a flyer he had picked up from one of the tourist brochure stands. It read "Hawai‘i Lifeguard Surf Instructors, Surfing Lessons." The catchy logo bore the red lifeguard cross with a couple of surfboards crisscrossed behind it and circled by a buoy.

CHAPTER SIX

Surf Lessons

This is not so easy as it looks. First you have to recognize the proper wave when it comes, and secondly, even more important, you have to know the wrong wave when it comes, because if that catches you and forces you down to the bottom, heaven help you!
—AGATHA CHRISTIE, *AN AUTOBIOGRAPHY*, 1977

Paulette, the boys, and I pulled into a driveway on Aliʻi Drive, the main strip which hugs the Kailua-Kona coast, and knocked on the beachfront bungalow door. A Hawaiian man about thirty, sporting geometrical Polynesian tattoos on his biceps, greeted us.

"Aloha. I'm Che. You must be the Conrad family." He led us through the surf shack to the back porch, which hung over the rocks of the shoreline and offered a clear view of the waves breaking on the reef. "Pretty big today. It's okay. We'll stay more on the inside."

At that moment, a kook (a novice or poser surfer), struggling against the current, was swept past the porch, certain to end up on the rocks. Che shouted to him to paddle out of the rip current, but the panicked and tired fellow did not understand.

"Geez, you can't believe it. We make at least one rescue a week here, and we're *retired* lifeguards," Che said.

He waved his hands at the lifeguard tower at Kahalu'u Beach Park and pointed at the potential drowning victim. One of the lifeguards paddled out on a twelve-foot-long orange board and pulled the man out of the riptide and into the safety of the lagoon. During the rescue, Che taught my sons how to paddle, get to their feet in a crouching position—arms extended out for balance—and ride the board.

While the boys changed into swim shorts and stowed their towels and clothes, I talked with Che. It turned out that he had sailed around the Hawaiian Islands on *Hawai'i Loa*,[8] a double-hull sailing canoe similar in design to the famous voyaging canoe *Hōkūle'a*, Hawaiian for "Star of Gladness," signifying Arcturus, which appears directly over the islands. The voyages were spiritually as well as scientifically significant for native Hawaiians as beginning in AD 300, the original settlers of Hawai'i arrived in similar sailing craft from the Tahitian and Marquesan Islands.

The *Hōkūle'a* project's purpose was to illustrate how the ancient Polynesians navigated by celestial observation and a profound knowledge of the currents, winds, cloud formations, and even the flight of seabirds. Historically, the individual islands of the South Pacific were not as isolated as some people think. For short distances, small paddling canoes were sufficient; for longer voyages, the double-hull sailing canoes, ranging in length from 30 feet up to an incredible 118 feet, traversed the Pacific at greater speed than the tall-masted and cumbersome European ships. Modern-day catamarans, which cruise all over the world, are based on the design of Polynesian sailing

---

8. *The vessel Hawai'i Loa was made of traditional materials for the most part, but it was also equipped with a satellite link that allowed the crew to talk on a daily basis with students in Hawaiian classrooms.*

canoes. *Hōkūle'a*[9] made round-trip voyages between Hawai'i and Tahiti in 1976 and 1980. She also traveled throughout Polynesia and down to New Zealand, the southernmost point of the Polynesian triangle, between 1985 and 1987.

I told Che that, in 1991, I had been in the Îles Sous-le-Vent, one hundred miles from Tahiti, at the same time *Hōkūle'a* sailed in, and I had met the voyagers. That day the surf was dangerous, at heights of up to ten feet (I was a real surfer then). I was "talking story" with one of the Hawaiian sailors on the beach, who turned out to be none other than Tiger Espere, a famous surfer of the seventies. I offered Tiger the use of my board, but he nodded at *Hōkūle'a*, bobbing in the turquoise lagoon.

"The boat. Can't do anything that might slow it down. You know, *kuleana*, responsibility," Tiger had answered. Accidents in this dangerous sport happen very quickly.

---

9. *In 2017, Hōkūle'a returned to Hawaii after a voyage around the world that took three years, spanned forty thousand nautical miles, and was completed entirely without the use of modern navigational instruments.*

"Tiger is my father's cousin," Che said enthusiastically.

"Cool."

"And you know we hold the Tiger Longboard Classic every year, near your new house at Kawaihae. Here, pick out any board you like," he said. With a generous sweep of his hand, he motioned toward the rack of boards.

I declined his gracious offer and rubbed my shoulder. "I haven't surfed in two years, not since my rotator cuff injury; maybe I'll kick around on a sponge," I said and grabbed one of the boogie boards leaning against the wall.

"Hey, if we keep talking story, I'll bet we find out we same family, cousins or something," he said with a jovial, brown toothy grin. "Let's surf." Out of the rack he chose a couple of beater boards for the boys. Then he, the boys, and I tucked the boards under our arms and goat-walked down a sandy trail on the roadside, passing the smallest chapel I had ever seen.

The trail ended at a tiny inlet between rocks that crawled with little black crabs. Che instructed Anthony and Will to drop their boards in the knee-deep water, lie down, and begin paddling. I put mine down on a slab of lava rock and ducked inside the small chapel for a moment. (Like bullfighters before they enter the ring, most avid surfers—even if they do not attend church regularly—make prayers of some kind before paddling into the almighty waters.) Inside was a glass etching of St. Peter helping fishermen out of the sea.

Sheltered by the outer reef, the waves were shapely. Che waved for me to move over to the left side of the horseshoe-shaped bay. He pushed my older son into a wave. Anthony stood up for a few seconds before toppling into the white foam, and Will rode a frothy white wall until he spilled. I paddled over and, eventually, we all three caught the same wave and were surfing together. The old thrill

was back, but it was better than ever for the exhilaration in my sons' eyes and the joyous grins on their faces.

After our wave, another large swell was bearing down on us. Che went for it himself, and I watched his technique. He paddled out vigorously, turned his board around, stroked into the six-foot wave, and swooped down the face and into the trough like an eagle. He arched his back gracefully just as the lip of the wave pitched over his head, and stood calmly as if taking an outdoor shower. His right arm pointed up to the crest of the wave, and his left was extended parallel to the board. He guided the board under the wave's force, making it look as easy as an afternoon stroll. Che has the estimable reputation on the Big Island of being an all-around waterman: swimming, sailing, canoe paddling, surfing. A few islanders refer to him as the Duke Kahanamoku[10] of the twenty-first century, an ambassador of the aloha spirit.

---

10. *Duke Kahanamoku (1890–1968) was the father of modern surfing. He won the Olympic gold medal in the one-hundred-meter freestyle swim at Stockholm in 1912 and again at Antwerp in 1920. He acted in Hollywood movies, was photographed for brochures promoting Hawai'i, and was sheriff of Honolulu for many years.*

Every morning, the boys and I looked out at the ocean from our third-floor hotel room to gauge if the wind was too strong. Then, after breakfast, we would drive down to the surf shack.

A few days after our first lesson, Che walked into the surf shack, back from the North Shore of O'ahu, his chest wrapped in bandages. "Ruptured spleen—stitches—fifteen-footer at Rocky Point," he explained.

Yes, big-wave riding is perilous. However, being in the smaller waves is refreshing and invigorating. And the effervescent bubbles, made from the energy of breaking waves, are said to be healthy for one's body and spirit. They go straight to the brain like nontoxic champagne, natural and restorative.

After our third lesson, back in our basic hotel room in the late afternoon, I was sunburned, exercised, and elated. I blurted, "This is just the kind of place where professional surfers stay while on the world circuit."

"Okay, Dad," said Anthony, now sixteen. "So where are the babes?"

CHAPTER SEVEN

Mele Kalikimaka

The sleepiest, quietest, Sundayest looking place you can imagine.
—MARK TWAIN, *ROUGHING IT IN THE SANDWICH ISLANDS*, 1866

Staying at Uncle Billy's in the heart of Kailua-Kona, we were able to watch the annual Christmas parade from its umbrella-covered poolside tables. There were a few ukulele players, but surprisingly, no hula dancers. If the participants had not been mainly Asians and Hawaiians belting out the salutation *Mele Kalikimaka* (Merry Christmas), we might have been in any small town in the United States.

Elks Lodge members, with fake antlers on their heads, walked behind a sports car with giant antlers affixed to its hood. The local churches sponsored floats with Nativity scenes, and the Humane Society paraded all the unwanted mutts on leashes, some also sporting horns on their furry heads. Only the cute high school cheerleaders were antlerless, shaking their pom-poms and waving shyly to the crowd.

On the afternoon of Christmas Eve, our house was ready and we were delighted with what we found as we pulled into its driveway. Lovelier than we had imagined, it seemed to be waiting for us like a bride with eyes downcast in anticipation of her groom's kiss. Its shiny new paint was a luminescent light green, and the cream trim looked like the icing on a Key lime pie.

It was too late to buy a Christmas tree—all the stores had sold out—so we set up an areca palm in the corner of our living room and strung up some lights before attending the service at Hokuloa Church, a mile away. The little chapel, built in 1860 by Reverend Lorenzo Lyons, an American Congregational missionary, was used until the closing of the Puako sugar plantation in 1914, and lingered on in disrepair until its restoration in 1990. It is said to have that special spirit of a holy place. Not being a pious parishioner made me

appreciate the candlelight service for its novelty. I had so much to be thankful for; I had my little family there together in the warmth of the islands—a blessing in themselves.

Some of the hymns were sung alternately in English and Hawaiian. Many of us carefully sounded out the Hawaiian words to "Silent Night."

Po-la'ie, po kama-ha'o,
Ma-lu-hia, ma-lama-lama
Ka ma-kua-hi-ne a-lo-ha e
Me ke kei-ki he-mo-lele e
Moe me ka ma-lu-hia la-ni

The volume was louder on the English stanza.

Then the pastor gave his sermon. In it, he said, "The church has distributed to needy families over 8,500 pounds of packaged food items, 2,000 pounds of rice, 101 turkeys and hams, 120 dozen eggs, 800 rolls of toilet paper, and 80 rubber slippers." Rubber slippers—not shoes—in the middle of winter. *Hawai'i is paradise even for the needy,* I thought.

The hard-blown whitecaps, visible from our balcony, looked like snow on that Christmas morning. After breakfast the boys opened their presents. Will twanged his new ukulele, anticipating that his new school would offer lessons. Both sons tore into boxes of fishing rods, reels, and tackle.

For the next few days, the boys spent hours fishing but mostly just hooked the reef. Anthony would cast out to sea, and when he got his lure snagged on the coral, he would send his little brother into the water to retrieve it. One day, little brother stepped on a sea urchin. Paulette removed the needles with tweezers. Following a time-tested Hawaiian remedy (and much against his protests), we had him soak his foot in a bowl of his urine to remove the toxins. Within a day he was scampering over the reef like *a'ama*, the dark crabs that inhabit the coast.

Weeks later the Matson container was deposited in our driveway with a loud clang. Three massive Hawaiians unloaded our furniture, paintings, boxes of books, kayak, bicycles, toys, tools, et cetera. Most of the stuff ended up in a big pile in the middle of my studio, like a permanent garage sale.

I worked in the studio every day on my stock photography business, catching up on sending out material. And what a studio it was, full of light. We set up easels and we all painted island scenes. Paulette drove up to Waimea and took Will to school, shopped for groceries, and ran errands—a break from years of a nine-to-five job. She had time to take yoga classes, garden, read novels, and go for long, leisurely walks—a welcome change from commuting to an office. International news had become less relevant to us. We got newspapers but didn't hook up cable; instead, we watched rented disks at night. Will's study habits improved and his grades went up.

The foundations of our house and the cottage were set on pilings on top of rock, over an anchialine pond. These ponds are unique to the leeward side of Hawai'i: they rise and fall with the tide, the ocean water flowing through tunnels beneath the lava and even the road that separates our house from the beachfront properties. Fresh water runs underground from the mountains, too, through lava tubes. The ancient Hawaiians called this sort of terrain *'āina momona*, "sweet or fertile land." Here they raised fish and crustaceans.

One evening during a full moon, the tides rose higher than I had ever seen before. Waves washed over the beach access, bringing sand and coral rocks onto the road. That night, to the thundering sound of the crashing surf, I dreamed that waves were lapping against the porch of the cottage. Indeed they were: in the morning I found our backyard was flooded with brackish water. No wonder the lending bank had required us to get flood insurance at an exorbitant price. Luckily, the house wasn't flooded that night. Would we eventually become like Venetians, mopping water off our floors as a way of life?

A couple of days after the unusual tides, I found things wiggling in the toilet—little fish swimming in the bowl. Somehow they had entered the pipes from the overflowing pond after Gus ran over our septic tank with "da Bob," the Bobcat tractor. There were disadvantages, we discovered, to living in a house below sea level.

The fish were one thing; the smell was another. We called the septic guy. "Be there in a couple of days," he said. "I'm pretty backed up." Occupational humor.

"So am I," I said.

In the meantime, the stench from the overflowing tank was so unbearable that, to stop the overflow, we dug a latrine in the back behind the kiawe and milo trees. Phew! At that moment, I thought, "Why couldn't I have settled for a Florida beach house, or a Swiss chalet? A place where everything functions and people show up on time." In this dismal mood I acknowledged that I had to pay the bills, but my photo book sales had slacked, investments weren't panning out, and if serious royalties and dividends didn't come through on time, we would have to abandon this place in the sun. I had about another eight months to survive or succumb.

After excavation, the pipes and the tank were resealed. A large invoice arrived. The toilet fish returned whence they'd come. The sun came out. The pond teemed with tilapia as well as the imported Japanese koi. A couple of opportunistic herons arrived and stood still on their chopstick legs like displays in a taxidermy shop. On occasion, they would rapidly dip their beaks into the water and reemerge holding silvery fish—maybe the ones from the toilet.

A flock of ducks fluttered their white feathers in the pond. I'm not sure where they came from, but they congregated on the porch, leaving droppings all over our wrought-iron chairs and benches, running wild, and squawking at odd times. We liked having them around; they ate bugs. At first there were five ducks, but then only four. One morning the neighbor's husky ran through our backyard with a limp duck in its mouth. Eventually, only one duck remained. We felt sorry for it and fed it pieces of bread, in effect adopting it. It slept under the house at night and paddled our pond during the day.

CHAPTER EIGHT

Our Island Garden

If you try, you will find me where the sky meets the sea.
Here am I your special island: Come to me, Come to me.
—RICHARD RODGERS, FROM "BALI HAI," *SOUTH PACIFIC*, 1949

The meandering bramble in our rear yard needed civilizing. At a Kona nursery, I picked out truckloads of dwarf coconut trees, ti plants, bougainvillea, and—my favorite tropical plant—the tiare gardenia (*gardenia taitensis*). This fragrant-smelling white flower, with six to eight cream-white petals, of the bush with floppy green leaves is the olfactory essence of the South Seas. The tiare Tahiti (as it is named on the island of Tahiti) has been growing in Hawai'i for as long as people can remember—perhaps since the first Hawaiian settlers journeyed from Tahiti, 2,800 miles to the south. The first pioneer women may have brought the plants along in the canoes as a comforting ornament, a sweet reminder of home in their new frontier island.

Lalamilo, our gardener, was a grizzled old man, an authentic Hawaiian, and was recommended to us by a neighbor. He showed up one day in the front yard wearing a torn aloha shirt. Perched on his head was a hat of woven pandanus fronds, the brim so frayed he looked like a scarecrow. In spite of his extended poi belly—evidence of many sumptuous luaus—he looked strong. His eyes hinted at Chinese descent, but his olive skin and bone structure indicated Polynesian lineage. He regally greeted me with *"Aloha oe, e komo mai i ka 'āina no Havai'i nui."* (Hello, welcome to the land of the great Hawai'i.) I tried a little Tahitian on him, but it didn't work, except for a few words like *opu* (stomach), *nui* (big), and *va'a* (canoe), which are the same in both languages. I realized that he was one of those rare Hawaiians who still spoke the beautiful and poetic native language. Lalamilo also spoke Pidgin and Pākē Hawaiian, a mixture of Pidgin English spoken by the early Chinese workers and a few scattered Hawaiian words.

Lalamilo told us not only about the flora and fauna but much about island life and aloha spirit. He came up with original sayings, and the first time he came to the property, he looked up at the newer back house and said, "So, Mister Haole built his *hale*. You be plenny *ha'oli*, happy, here, once we make da kine garden fo' you." The way he called me *haole*, foreigner, was not demeaning, as the term can sometimes be used, but just a matter of fact. And I liked him immediately for his linguistic hijinks.

Haole literally means "without breath" in Hawaiian. When Captain Cook and his men sailed to Hawai'i, the Hawaiians called them *haole*, possibly because they couldn't speak the Polynesian language. Or was it because they looked sickly—without breath? For the most part, the sailors were typical of that period—malnourished, travel-weary, flea-infested, alcoholic, and ravaged by venereal disease.

"Me, I am *kanaka maoli*," Lalamilo said to me one day. He threw his shoulders back proudly. The term *kanaka* or *kanak* has had a derogatory stigma attached to it dating back to the days of whaling, white traders, and pirates of the South Seas, but it literally means "man of Polynesia." In New Caledonia they call themselves *kanaks* and in Tahiti *taata maohi*. In New Zealand, the southern tip of the Polynesian Islands triangle, they call themselves Maori. The roots of the Polynesian words are quite often the same, but the prefixes and the suffixes are different from island to island. A few letters here and there, and many of the words are similar—just as the Romance languages are all related and based on Latin. For instance, *enua* ("land," in Marquesan) is *fenua* in Tahitian and *'āina* in Hawaiian. But in Tahitian a *kaina* is someone of the land or from the countryside; in Hawaiian it is *kama'āina*. *Fare* means "house" in Tahitian; in Samoan it is *fale*; and in Hawaiian it is *hale*. *Wahine* is "woman" in Hawaiian; the Tahitian is similar, *vahine*. In Tahiti, "hello" is *ia ora na*; in the Cook Islands it is *kiaorana*, and in the Tuamotus it is *kiaora*—the same as in the Maori language of New Zealand. Moving north to the Marquesas, it becomes *kaoha*, and of course in Hawai'i, aloha. For all my knowledge, *aloha* and *mahalo* were the only Hawaiian words I used effectively, so I bought the best book on the language: *Hawaiian Dictionary* by Mary Kawena Pukui and Samuel H. Elbert. Certainly, I wouldn't become fluent, but I wanted to know a few dozen words, or maybe a hundred. Like the word for "goodness" (*pono*) or "mischievous" (*kolohe*). Learning a few words was not that hard; I just had to remember to pronounce all the vowels.

I learned that the Hawaiian language uses thirteen letters: the vowels *a, e, i, o, u*; the consonants *h, k, l, m, n, p, w*; and the *ʻokina* (ʻ), which is a brief guttural break or glottal stop, sounding somewhat like a grunt. It is similar to the way an Englishman speaking with a Cockney accent would say "bu'er" and not "butter." The guttural break is important, as a word with or without it can completely change the meaning. Take for instance these three words, all spelled similarly but with very different meanings depending on the pronunciation: *ʻaʻi* means "neck," *ʻai* means "food," and *ai* means "sexual intercourse." And so with this phonetic language, mistakes on the accents can land one in hot water, as they had me with Luana, the insurance agent.

Many words have no consonants, and all syllables end with a vowel. Basically, *a* is pronounced "ah" as in *father*. *E* is pronounced "a" as in *apple*. Often *i* is pronounced as "ee." Hawaiian articulation is based largely at the back of the tongue, while English relies on the tip. Generally, verbs precede their subjects, and nouns precede their adjectives.

It wasn't long before I could understand that lovely song on the radio, "E Huli Ho 'i Mai." It means "Turn around and come back."

Soon, I began the mornings greeting Lalamilo with *"E komo mai"* (Come in, welcome), and during one of our numerous conversations, Lalamilo asked me if I knew the real meaning of *aloha*. I didn't. "*Aloha* means," he said, "the holy breath of life." He explained that *alo* means "to be in the presence of," and *ha* is "the divine breath of life." "Alo-o-haaa," he said and looked up to the sky. "Da earth, da sky, moon, smell of flowers in da garden, and salt of da sea." He breathed in deeply. "*Haaa*, the breath of life. It gives me da kine cheeken skeen," he said, pointing at the goose bumps on his arm, "just to think how *nani*"—beautiful—"it is." Then he stopped talking. As I got to know him, I learned that Lalamilo's loneliness was expressed two ways: too much chatter or a loss for words. He drifted between the two.

Lalamilo taught us all about the plants of Hawai'i and shared island lore passed down through many generations, including tales of Pele, a goddess of creation and destruction with red hair and fiery lava eyes. Aided by a crew of Hawaiians, he also created our garden, but the installation progressed at glacial speed. When we left for any period of time, we'd notice, upon our return, that not a soul was to be seen. The workers would scurry away, like mongooses disappearing into the jungle. Over a handful of mornings, however, trucks delivered a full twenty tons of dirt and gravel and slabs of cut lava rock, for stepping-stones and a barbecue area. The garden slowly took shape. Every day it became *nani*, lovelier. The miniature plumeria trees blossomed, along with the pink and scarlet hibiscus. And we put in sprigs of grass, and before long I was yoked behind the handles of my new Honda. Not a motorcycle, but a lawn mower, the symbol of suburbia, the very place I had escaped from. I loathed that obnoxious noise, but our grass became a pure suede of an English green, and we began chipping golf balls, swishing badminton rackets, belting with croquet mallets, and kicking soccer balls.

One night, however, I heard a strange rustling and grunting in the yard. I shone a flashlight; to my horror, there was a herd of wild hogs rooting. In the beam of the light, I counted sixteen pigs engrossed with their snouts rooting in *our* lawn. They didn't notice me walk out. But I yelled at them to shoo them away. A couple of the largest hogs just stared back at me and snorted. *Whoa!* I backed off. These beasts meant business.

I called Lalamilo and asked him what to do. He said, "I t'ink of somet'ing. Heh, you go star gaz'n, no fall asleep in lawn chair back der, yah."

"Why?" I said.

"Eat chew up. They'll eat anyt'ing. Ram you with der tusks."

In the meantime, half the lawn turned into rubble, worse than when we'd started our garden. The irrigation hoses and sprinklers were mangled and exposed. We went to Honolulu for the weekend, and when we returned home we inspected the lawn: no signs of further damage. At night, no more sounds of grunting. The next time Lalamilo showed up, I asked him how he got rid of the wild hogs.

"Dogs and then . . ." He pantomimed, pumping his arm up and down with his fist closed as if holding a machete.

"Soon, we have kalua pork," he said with a smile.

One day I heard Lalamilo singing verses of a rhyme, which I thought was Lear's "The Owl and the Pussycat." But listening more closely, I heard the words *ule* and *pupule*. "What's that you're humming?" I asked.

"Oh, just one silly rhyme fo' *keiki*—children."

I begged him to sing it again, and he blushed and said it was very naughty. He paused, then said, "Well, okay." He grinned sheepishly and looked over his shoulder as if a neighbor might appear to chastise him.

"Der was an ol' man from Waipahu.
Who played all day long with his laho.
He wen' go pupule *from pulling his* ule,
Dat crazy ol' man from Waipahu."

I knew that Waipahu was a district near Pearl Harbor, where I'd bought my truck at a strip known as "auto row." I already knew that *ule* meant "penis," and that *pupule* meant "crazy." But I didn't know what *laho* meant. I checked my new dictionary: "scrotum." So much for luau limericks.

Another day Lalamilo said, "You know what our state motto is? *Ua mau ke ea o ka 'āina i ka pono*. It means 'The life of the land is perpetuated in righteousness.' But dat's *lolo*, 'cause here like doorway to all the Pacific, and through it come all kine *pupule* people, yah," he said.

"Yeah, in California, lots of weirdos end up there, as it's the end of the continent. Then they come over here," I said.

"You know when I was young and wen' go Waikīkī, some of da beach boys say da state motto der is *Hele haole lolo, hoi mai kala*. It mean 'Go away, you crazy *haole*, but bring back money.'" He cackled. Then he held up his right hand at eye level and rubbed his thumb together with his forefinger and middle finger and said, "Speaking of *kala* . . ." With his left hand, he handed me a bill for his work.

Often we talked about favorite island foods, such as marlin poke—raw cubed fish with *limu* (seaweed). One day I asked Lalamilo what was the most exotic dish he had ever tried. Pensively, he looked up at a coconut tree and said, "I got lots of Flip friends—you know, Filipinos. Dey like dog. Not like you and I like dog, but fo' *kaukau*." He made a motion with his hand as if holding a fork and shoveling food off a plate. "I try dog at der luau. Taste same like *pua'a*, wild pig like the ones I got there." He pointed toward the bushes in the back.

I could not stop laughing, so he came up with another one: "Dere lots of Korean in Hawai'i, but when dey wok da dog, it no mean same t'ing. *Wok*, yah."

Some years ago, the state legislature, pushed by animal rights groups, proposed a bill that would ban the slaughter of dogs for food. Several members of Asian groups protested that the measure gave credence to a racist stereotype of their culture, as their forebears had settled in Hawai'i several generations before, and the eating of dog meat was repugnant to them.

CHAPTER NINE

Some Sharks Bite

*E ao o pau poʻo, pau hiʻu ia mano. (Be careful
lest you go head and tail into the shark.)*
—MARY KAWENA PUKUI, ʻOLELO NOʻEAU: HAWAIIAN
PROVERBS AND POETICAL SAYINGS, 1983

From the book *Sharks of Hawaiʻi*, I learned that there are attacks in
this archipelago every year, and the author, Leighton Taylor, provided
a register of the 101 shark attacks recorded between 1779 and 1992.
I wondered how many bloody thrashings followed these, and how
many more there would be.

Case number two was recorded in 1828 at Lahaina, Maui: *"A man
out riding surf at ʻUo was killed by a shark which bit off his limbs and
left his body floating." Attack witnessed by a number of Hawaiian chiefs.*

Case number seven, in 1904, Honolulu, Oʻahu, was of an unnamed
male: *Partial remains of swimmer who had disappeared two days earlier
off Diamond Head found in the stomach of a "monstrous shark." Body*

was complete from the waist down with the exception of one leg. Shark also contained ducks, tin cans, and wood.

Case number forty-two, on 13 December 1958 in Lanikai, Oʻahu, was of a William S. Weaver: *Leg amputated while surfing on an air mattress near Mokulua Islands; 15-to 25-ft shark (believed to be a tiger shark) observed near body when fire-rescue personnel recovered it 2 hours later. No additional bite marks present on the body.* Coincidentally, I knew the victim's uncle, Spencer Weaver, a hotel financier, and I was a friend of the victim's cousin "Spinner."

I used to swim at many of the locations of the brutal attacks; it could have been *me.* I rubbed the skin on my back and knocked on wood.

The book explained that the ancient Hawaiians' lives were intertwined with sharks'; they believed that deceased relatives could become beneficent guardian spirits called *ʻaumakua,* taking the form of animals such as owls, sea turtles, eels, and sharks. These family protectors and fishing helpers did the bidding of the kahuna, or caretaker. Fables are associated with the *ʻaumakua.* At times, they changed from man to beast like werewolves of European myth. The old legend of Kapaʻaheo, the Kohala shark god, recorded in the Bishop Museum archives, is especially werewolfesque.

Long ago young girls enjoyed swimming in a lovely cove in Kohala on the Big Island. Often a swimmer would disappear and never be seen again. The people were very afraid and wanted to learn what had happened to the girls. A fisherman noticed that when a swimmer disappeared, a mysterious stranger named Kapaʻaheo could be seen sitting on the shore nearby. This fisherman then got all of the other fishermen together, and they were on hand when the girls went swimming again. As before, the stranger was sitting on the rocks overlooking the cove. When he disappeared, the leader of the fishermen ordered the others to dive into the water and form a protective circle around the girls. The shark swam toward the group, and a huge fight began. Many times the shark was wounded by the spears of the fishermen. Finally the shark swam away. When the men were back on the shore, they found the stranger dying from many wounds that looked like they were made by fishing spears. When the man died from the wounds, he was transformed into the stone found near the edge of the cliff of the ocean.

That nine-foot lava stone was moved from near the Upolu Airport to the Bishop Museum in Honolulu, where today it is set in a lovely garden. (There is a rumor that you can still hear the scream of a young Hawaiian girl if you put your ear next to the stone on the night of a full moon. *Auwe*, cheeken skin!)

Fifteen miles south of our *hale* is the Kona Village Resort, an old-time getaway spot where one pays *not* to have a telephone or a TV in the room. One hundred twenty-five bungalows surrounded by coconut trees are set on lava rocks and sited around ponds, like ours, overlooking the ocean. The thatched roofs give the appearance of a traditional Polynesian village. But there are no scrawny chickens, mud-caked pigs, or mangy yellow dogs. Just mai tai–slurping *haole* minding their sunburns and rum intake.

After winding through a series of sandy paths, we arrived at the Bora Bora Bar, where my octogenarian father and stepmother sat nursing their cocktails and looking out at the small bay. Dad and Mary had been staying there every Thanksgiving for thirty years; in this tranquil setting, some of the employees and fellow guests have become like family. My father was a professional artist, and many of his commissioned portraits of seasoned employees adorn the walls.

With drinks in hand, we were viewing the sunset when one of the beach boys ran up the seaside path. With his eyes bulging out like a big-eyed tuna's, he frantically yelled, "Somebody call 9-1-1! Shark attack!"

Lifeguards manned a dinghy and pulled a fifty-year-old woman, a guest at the hotel, aboard—bloody, but very much alive. They carried her onto the beach, wrapped her in towels (instantly soaked with blood), and drove her to the heliport in the nearby black lava fields. We heard the *thuk, thuk, thuk* of a helicopter landing at the Village's old airport (the resort's only access, except for those traveling by boat, before the coast road was built in 1975). The poor woman was medevaced to the Kona hospital; the shark had taken off half her buttock and a couple of fingers.

Swimming was out until our anxieties about the attack had subsided. But, considering the population of water enthusiasts where we live, the chances of being hit by a shark are lower than of being struck by lightning. Soon I was back in the water, surfing every chance I had—some days with crowds, others with only a handful of surfers at secret spots, and occasionally alone.

One solo windy afternoon, I was sitting on my board waiting for a wave about three hundred yards offshore when I felt something pass beneath the surface. From the top of a wave, a dark fin popped out of the water. I froze like a deer staring into the headlights of a truck full of hillbilly hunters. I instinctively pulled my hands and feet out of the water. *Be cool.*

Then, as fast as the fin had appeared, it submerged. Was it the same shark that had bitten the woman at the Kona Village, coming back for another medium-rare buttock? Now what, turn the other cheek?

I started to paddle in, slowly at first. Then rapidly. I thought of the old saying "Reach with your left arm, stroke, and say, 'Some sharks bite.' Then reach with your right and say, 'Some sharks don't.'"

Once on the beach, I counted my blessings along with my fingers, and I reflected that I didn't know what kind of shark it was. Of the 350 species, I knew it wasn't a whale shark,[11] the largest shark in the world, exceeding thirty feet in length. Nor was it a megamouth,[12] with its three-foot-wide silver-lined mouth reflecting light to attract tiny shrimp in deep, dark waters. And it wasn't a cookiecutter shark, recognizable by its cigar-shaped body and short snout, which preys on fish much larger than itself by masquerading as bait and then swimming vertically toward the surface, biting and rotating its body like a drill, and stealing a plug of flesh about the size of a small cookie. I rubbed my belly—still all there—having already seen the circular bites on the undersides of ono while deep-sea fishing.

As I walked back along the seaside trail, I thought, *It was probably the most common, the whitetip or the blacktip reef sharks,* mano pa'ele—*biters, but not too aggressive.* Then I scared myself: *Maybe it was one of the big boys—the* niuhi, *the tiger or the great white.* Yes, there are great white sharks in Hawai'i. Quite often Californians and Australians stand on the beach and tell Hawaiians, "You're so lucky. Where *we* come from, we have a shark called 'the great white.'"

---

11. *The whale shark, the friendly shark, is known in Hawai'i as lele wa'a, meaning "flying canoe." These special sharks have been known to lean on outrigger canoes for handouts of food. They are so docile, divers can hang on to their fins to hitch a ride.*
12. *The first megamouth shark ever discovered was caught off O'ahu by a research vessel in 1976. It was named the Megachasma pelagios, Greek for "giant yawner of the sea."*

Many Hawaiians just smile and politely nod, not wishing to ruin the *malahinis'* vacation by saying the great whites are in Hawai'i, too. In ancient Hawai'i, the teeth of the great whites were used for cutting tools and weapons. Captain Cook returned to London with great white teeth. There have been eleven recordings of great whites in Hawai'i since 1874, and there have been two attacks—one fatal. Predators of sea lions and seals, great whites were more common when there was a larger population of monk seals on the islands.

A few months after my shark sighting, I read in the newspapers that a diver left the protection of a shark cage and swam with an eighteen-foot great white. He even touched it as he snapped photos. Rather daring!

Most of the attacks are from the tigers, which are territorial and also mistake swimmers for turtles, their main food source. However, they'll eat anything: floating seabirds, lobsters, garbage. Trash can lids have been found in their stomachs.

One key difference between a great white and a tiger is that the latter will back off from a fight, or tire out after a bite. In fact, big tigers can be handled when well fed, as one fisherman proved when he opened Marineland almost sixty years ago. People flocked to the outskirts of Honolulu to see young Hawaiians ride upon their backs. The "sharkquarium" is long gone, but the University of Hawai'i houses bottlenose porpoises in the tanks as part of a research program on cetacean communication.

In 1991 and 1992, several shark attacks, including two fatalities, prompted the state to start fishing programs to catch tiger sharks near popular beach areas. The thirteen-to-fifteen-foot sharks, hanging from hooks on the docks, brought crowds of gawkers, and photos of the catches were featured on the front pages of newspapers. Some objected to these programs because of the complexity of ancient

Hawaiian lore regarding *'aumakua*. However, there is dissent among Hawaiians on this. In *The Honolulu Advertiser*, on the topic of a shark being someone's *'aumakua*, Rona Kaaekuahiwi, a canoe coach, was quoted as saying, "Those things went out with Kamehameha. What kind of books are they reading? Let it be one of their children."

After surfing, while I was hosing off my surfboard in the carport one afternoon, I asked Lalamilo what his thoughts were on catching the sharks. He said, "As Buffalo Keaulana, the famous surfer and lifeguard from the Wai'anae coast, once said, 'We respect the sharks, but we should fish for them when there is an attack.'"

He leaned on his rake and said, "*'Aumakua*, important. Have *'aumakua* in da *pueo*, in da *honu*, and in da plants and da stones. But *auwe*! You beddah off no shaak bite *okole*, yah."

"*Shaak bait* is Pidgin for tourist. But local surfers and spear fishermen get chomped too," Lalamilo continued. He appeared to communicate with the clouds and reverently looked skyward when asked a question, as if looking into his people's mysterious past. He turned to me, seeming to report his ancestors' opinion.

"What you t'ink? We no catch shaak befo'? Old days catch 'em plenny, eat 'em like steak. Use da skeen fo' drum, use da *niho* fo' knife." He went on to say "We should catch 'em near the swimming beaches, and as my grandfadder say from old Bible, in Hawaiian, '*He maka no ka maka, he niho no ka niho.*' Eye for an eye, tooth for a tooth."

He added that he missed eating *honu* from when he was a boy and that the Hawaiians should be able to eat some of the turtles. "Have *honu* hunting season. Like over dere *'aina haole* you got deer tags."

One week after my shark encounter, a friend of mine was kayaking a mile off the coast. He jumped into the ocean for a cool dip and was hanging on to the kayak, dangling his lower body in the water, when he felt something hit his buttock. Thinking it was a turtle or a porpoise, he turned around to see the head of a shark, two feet wide. (They sometimes bump their prey before circling around for the attack.) He flew out of the water and into his kayak and watched the greenish-gray glow of a ten-foot tiger shark glide by. Normally, this laid-back long-haired friend of mine would paddle slowly while leisurely observing the fish and seabirds. But on that day, some of the canoe team paddlers swore they had watched a potential Molokaʻi race champion streak to shore as fast as a shooting star. Once on the beach, he wept, and for days he couldn't stop shaking. That shocking experience must have rearranged his neurons; thereafter, he always paddled at a brisk pace.

Over the years, the newspapers reported many attacks: swimmers were hit just off Maui; a bodyboarder off Kauaʻi lost his lower leg; a surfer was bitten on the arm near the old airport in Kailua, and then another was slashed in the foot at Kahaluʻu Beach Park, where my boys had taken their surf lessons. In 2015, a doctor was mauled in the middle of the day a few miles from our house, at Hapuna Beach—our "safe" swimming spot. In 2012, there were nine shark attacks. In 2013, there were fourteen, three times the normal.

On Halloween 2003, headline news around the world reported that thirteen-year-old Bethany Hamilton's left arm had been bitten off four inches below her shoulder. The attack occurred at 7:30 a.m. at Tunnels, on the north shore of Kauaʻi. Bethany was surfing with her friend Alana Blanchard, also thirteen, when the twelve-foot shark attacked. Alana's father, Holt, used a surf leash as a tourniquet. She lost half her blood supply and blacked out briefly before making it to Wilcox Hospital. Incredibly, the victim's father, Tom Hamilton, was on the operating table awaiting a knee operation when a doctor burst in and said that they needed the operating room for a thirteen-year-old shark attack victim. When Tom heard that, he knew it was either his daughter or her friend.

A week later, while awaiting the removal of her stitches, Bethany bravely said, "If I was like a person that just quit surfing after this, I wouldn't be a real surfer. I'm definitely going to get back in the water." A few months later, she was surfing again, saying that if it was God's wish, so be it. This nice girl didn't even want the shark harmed. But a neighbor went on a bender, got a boat, and went out to sea like the trio in *Jaws*; he caught and killed the shark.

In Florida, thirty attacks occured in 2016. But as an old *kama‘āina* told me, "Those Florida sharks are nippers. Our little sharks behave. It's the big ones to watch out for."

CHAPTER TEN

Wrestling with the Sea

That is what it is, a royal sport for the natural kings of earth.
—JACK LONDON, *THE CRUISE OF THE SNARK*, 1911

Most water accidents involve drowning, which in the islands primarily befalls tourists. Hawai'i has the most drownings per capita of any state. About one person a week perishes in the rip currents and treacherous surf, or is simply blown by high winds out to sea in small craft. Many people do not heed or follow lifeguards' advice on ocean conditions.

In any case, I couldn't stay out of the water, especially one fall day while driving down the road from Waimea. I saw white lines stretching across the ocean. A trail of froth, like whipped cream, appeared where the waves broke on the reef outside of Kawaihae Harbor. I turned onto a sand and coral gravel road, followed it for about a half mile down to the sea, parked, and got out. On the beach, I found a shipping container with a porch and a small garden, upright oblong rocks, and a plaque with the words "The Life Saving Surfing Club" and *"Pua Ka 'ilima 'O Kawaihae."* The Hawaiian name came from the small island that once stood at that spot and the *'ilima* flower that flourished there. Looking southward, I saw a multitude of stones piled up to form a flat-topped pyramid with various graded levels. It was there, Pu'ukohola Heiau, that Kamehameha I unified the Hawaiian Islands with his mighty army and skilled navy. According to legend, a revered kahuna told the king that he had to build an impressive stone temple to receive enough *mana* from the gods, especially the war god, Ku, to enable him to conquer all of the islands.

In this cultural surf park with tremendous *mana*, a favorite of old watermen who love the ocean sports, I sat on one of the large boulders by the water and waxed up my board. Half a dozen surfers were riding the breakers in the same place where the king himself once surfed. I was encouraged by Jack London's words: "Get in and wrestle with the sea; wing your heels with the skill and power that reside in you; bit the sea's breakers, master them, and ride upon their backs as a king should."

London spent five months in Hawai'i and chronicled his South Seas voyage in *The Cruise of the Snark*. He surfed the long south swells of Waikīkī with passion.

I stepped down the stairs over the rocks, stroked through the turquoise water, and thanked the ancient Polynesians for inventing this adventure—*he'e nalu*, surfing—practiced for a thousand years. In ancient times the shortboard, *paipo*, up to four feet in length, was used for bodyboarding. The *alaia* ranged from seven to twelve feet, and the *olo* was up to sixteen feet and was reserved for kings. When the missionaries gained control in the 1800s, they banned surfing. Scantily clad natives having so much fun *had* to be sinful. A few continued to surf clandestinely; the sport survived and was revived at the turn of century. Ironically, today many surfers and board builders are pious Christians.

Carefully testing my shoulder, hoping the ligaments would hold up, I noticed that whoever caught a wave rode it to shore and then got out. Incredibly, I had the place to myself. A medium-sized, shapely wave came my way, and as I paddled for it, my shoulder made a cracking and popping sound—years of calcium deposits unfroze. I caught the wave and, during the next hour, rode a dozen more with ease and agility as if I had never left the sport. Apparently, it had never left me; I was as thrilled as when I was a seven-year-old boy surfing for the first time in Waikīkī.

Surfing has been a salve to my soul ever since my father built a beach house at Rincon Point near Santa Barbara, a place elegized by The Beach Boys. There wasn't a fine line between surfing and religion for me growing up on the beach, as my parents didn't go to church. Surfing was *righteous*. As a youngster, I dragged an old Hansen longboard across the barnacle-covered rocks and rode the long waves until I turned purple in the cold water. In my early twenties, I spent a season at Honolua Bay, Maui, and another year on Oʻahu. Then six years surfing in Tahiti, the mecca of soul surfing and the birthplace of the sport. For two years I just surfed, sailed, and fished in the leeward Society Islands. It was there, almost 250 years ago, in 1769, that Captain Cook recorded the sight of over two hundred people surfing those same waves.

Captain Cook had once sailed past Puako to Kawaihae, but because of high surf and lack of adequate anchorage, he didn't stay long. And there I was in the same place, surfing those waves, which only break during an extreme northwest swell. Being the only person in the water, except for a few kids on the inside, seemed like a miracle. I rode the long waves until I was too tired to paddle anymore, but it was just the inspiration needed to spur me to surf every time the swell came up that winter. Sometimes I crossed miles of black lava fields in temperatures over one hundred degrees in search of the perfect waves; but on most surf days, I'd just park my truck at the end of our street and walk down the trail along the shore for about a mile. Along the way I would pass the aptly named "Suicides"—the wave ends on the razor-sharp lava rocks. (Surf spots always have names given by surfers, and they're passed down generation to generation.) I kept a log. That year, I recorded twenty-five surf days and averaged about twenty waves each session. That's five hundred fun-filled waves. The greatest summer I ever had was that winter in Hawai'i.

The following surf seasons would be much the same except when Anthony, on Christmas break from boarding school, was my surf buddy. Will enthusiastically surfed the small waves of the shore break. (Phil Edwards, the famous surfer of the 1960s, once said, "The best surfer out there is the one having the most fun.")

On one of our many surf expeditions, I wiped out, and the ten-foot wave pulled me down to the bottom. Out of air, I pushed off the coral reef with my foot—*Ow!*—and surfaced with my arms pointed upward so as not to get hit on the head by the board or its fins. I took a deep breath and found my board next to me, now the size of a boogie board. I swam over and picked up the other broken half. As I awkwardly swam in, an old Hawaiian saying came to mind: "Don't paddle out if you can't swim in."

Shortboards, midlength, and longboards: most avid surfers have several boards—a "quiver." I'd choose one depending on the conditions in the same way a golfer pulls a club out of his bag. At the tight reef spots where the waves suck up the water, exposing the

coral, I would choose a shortboard, which facilitates turning inside the cylinder-shaped wave—another world, where time seems to lengthen. In small waves the longboard makes it easier to catch them, ride longer, walk the nose, and have "the most fun."

My only souvenir of these exhilarating days is a journal:

May 1, Honokohau Harbor

First time at this spot. Caught a lot of insiders, then moved out to catch the sets. Thick eight-foot barrels caught me! I thought I was going to break another board. Lucky. But it ended up getting dinged while getting on shore. Sharp lava rocks cut my foot.

December 15, Breakwall

I put Will on the mini-tank, and I rode his shortboard so it would be easier for him. We rode many waves together; he would turn to the left-hand side as he is a "goofy foot," and I would go right. He is quickly learning to surf. We saw Che paddle out, and he told us that he quit giving lessons. "I am an artist now—designs, everything. You want one these"— he pointed to his tattoo—"come on down to our gallery." Then he politely complimented his former student and said, "He got da style, brah."

In winter, storms from the Aleutian Islands or from Japan cause the waves to rumble thunderously as they crash on the reef. Often at night I was awakened by the siren's song, and was filled with both anticipation of riding the boasting waves and fear of a wipeout. Coral and rocks can rip you up or knock you out. When I was twelve years old, one of my friends, little Jeffrey Dodge, was surfing off Diamond Head. Nobody knew if he hit his head on his board or the shallow reef, but he died, and his death haunted me throughout my teenage years.

When I was twenty-six, another friend, Jean-Marc, a French architect, was hit by lightning at a remote reefbreak. A couple of his fellow surfers, who were also caught in the electrical storm, fetched his lifeless floating body. With surf leashes, they tied him onto his board and pulled him to shore. His skin had a deep-purple hue to it. His gold earring was still attached to his earlobe. Paramedics arrived, and he was pronounced dead.

CHAPTER ELEVEN

Night Marchers

Just as my aunt saw the marchers coming through the door, she snatched my brother away. As they went by, he tried to catch one of the legs of a fisherman, but the night marcher lifted his leg higher and kept marching. . . . I myself have seen it.
—SUSANNA MOORE, *I MYSELF HAVE SEEN IT: THE MYTH OF HAWAI'I*, 2003

Ominous clouds were gathering on the horizon five miles down the road from our Big Island *hale*. A few of us were surfing excellent waves until it began to rain in sheets and the lightning spurred us to shore. I was the last one on the beach at dusk. I walked through the coconut groves and took refuge at the poolside bar of a nearby resort. Monday Night Football was on the television, and the bartender poured a frothy beer from the tap. A mug of hops warmed my wet body.

The rain stopped and I made my way down the seaside coral trail, but by then it was pitch dark. After a wrong turn toward the lava fields, I couldn't see a thing. Suddenly, it seemed as if a trapdoor opened, and I fell into a hidden cellar. I let go of my surfboard; with a loud clang it landed on the lava floor, and my head bashed against a rock. Dazed for a moment, I realized that I'd fallen into a lava tube. I tried to move, but I felt a stinging stab in my back—sharp lava rocks piercing my flesh. I'd forgotten my mini flashlight, but there was an orange glow over the rim of the hole, and I crawled up the rocky precipice. Then I saw them.

Night marchers! Their torches were heading down to the sea. I knew from the stories not to stare directly into their dreaded eyes as they were thought to be capable of snatching souls away.

I was familiar with the book *I Myself Have Seen It*, a vivid collection of various Hawaiians' accounts of night marcher encounters by Susanna Moore. One Moloka'i resident saw them in 1958 and said, "The chanting came closer and closer. The first man was tall and strong, of the chief's class. All of them carried torches, but the light did not shine on their faces, only on their bodies and legs. 'They will go down to the beach, following a pathway in a straight line,' I said. 'They will not turn to the right or to the left.' And so it was."

Holy shit. I ducked my aching head under the rim of the lava tube. "Hide" was what one book had suggested; then, the night marchers, the phantom spirits, would pass. I sang a stanza of "Silent Night" in Hawaiian, the lyrics of which I remembered from Christmas Eve at the Hokuloa Church. *"Po la'i e, Po kama-ha'o, Ie-su i kou ha-nau 'a-na."* (Silent night, holy night, Jesus, Lord, at thy birth.)

Not only did I not want my soul to be snatched and sent to hell, I hoped to be spared the wrath of the night marchers' fiery gaze. There was already a large bump on my skull from its abrasive encounter with the lava rock. But then I thought, *What the hell, I'm probably going there anyway.* So I popped my head out and took my chances;

I looked directly at the night marchers, their torches lighting up the darkness with a fiery red glow. A zombie transformation, as in science fiction movies, seemed imminent as I stared at the flames. I crawled out of the tube, rubbed my eyes, and saw them all too clearly: dancers performing in a tourist luau at the resort.

Blood dripped from scratches on my head and lower back as I walked down the trail. Back home, never was a shower so embracing, a glass of red wine so warmly welcomed, and a dinner so appetizing. Through a gap in the flower-patterned drapes, I watched the raindrops fall into our dark garden and didn't even try to explain to Paulette what my afternoon had been like, as being from the islands she is naturally superstitious.

I hopped into bed holding an ice pack to the side of my head. Paulette giggled. "How about a little horizontal hula?"

"No mattress surfing. I have a headache." For once, it was the truth.

CHAPTER TWELVE

Castaways and Shipwrecks

Amongst the articles which they brought to barter . . . we
could not help taking notice of a particular sort of cloak
. . . nearly of the size and shape of the short cloaks worn
by the women in England, and by the men in Spain.
—CAPTAIN JAMES COOK, *THE VOYAGES OF CAPTAIN COOK*, 1778

At our annual community association meeting, I met history buff
Robby Robertson, a part-Hawaiian graduate of Punahou and UC
Berkeley. It was Robby who turned me on to the history of Hawaiian
encounters with European explorers. I was already reading Emmett
Cahill's *The Life and Times of John Young*, in part about the *Fair
American*, the tender ship to the *Eleanora*, an American brig sailing
from the northwest American coast to China for trade. In 1790,
Hawaiians seized the ship, and in the ensuing battle, all were killed
except for one man, Isaac Davis. A few years earlier, an American

sailing tyrant, Simon Metcalfe, who dealt in the profitable sandal-wood trade, massacred over a hundred natives on Maui after they stole a small boat from his schooner. Before the massacre, Metcalfe stopped at a village on beautiful Ka'upulehu Bay, where the Kona Village Resort now stands, and struck Kame'eiamoku—the right-hand man of Kamehameha I. The proud Hawaiian vowed vengeance on the next ship to show itself, which happened to be the *Fair American*, a fifty-four-foot schooner captained by none other than Thomas Metcalfe—Simon's son. Kame'eiamoku wanted payback. A new ship with weapons would restore his *mana*.

The chief boarded the schooner with a contingent of warriors on the pretext of trading, jumped Thomas and his five-man crew, tossed them overboard, and commanded his men to beat them to death with clubs as they dog-paddled in the water near the canoes.

Only one escaped, the first mate, Isaac Davis. "Isaac Davis was my grandfather going back seven generations," Robby told me. "He was a thirty-four-year-old Welshman when he arrived and eventually married a Hawaiian named Nakai. He subsequently married one of Kamehameha's nieces."

Between sips of lemonade at the picnic tables outside of the Hokuloa Church, which also serves as our community center, Robby explained Davis's escape. "A strong swimmer, he made his way toward shore, but he was caught by a canoe full of Hawaiians, who beat him on the head in the water, pulled him into the canoe, and were finishing the job by choking him to death. The leader admired Davis's fighting abilities and saved the half-drowned, bloody, and bruised sailor."

I knew from the book that the Hawaiians had hidden away the *Fair American* when the *Eleanora* sailed into Kawaihae Bay, but seven miles from my house. The *Eleanora* dropped anchor, and John

Young, a not-so-young boatswain at age forty-seven, went ashore to take a look around. Fearing that Young might discover the schooner, Kamehameha had his men detain Young, and the *Eleanora* sailed without him.

Isaac Davis and John Young eventually made their peace with Kamehameha, the George Washington of Hawai'i, and built up his navy by captaining the *Fair American*, his flagship, helping to unify the islands. "Davis was about to warn Kaumuali'i, ruler of Kaua'i, of an assassination plot," Robby told me, "when he himself was mysteriously poisoned in Honolulu, in 1810."

Kamehameha rewarded John Young with a homestead in direct view of Pelekane, the royal residence during the construction of the great *heiau* Pu'ukohola. For forty-five years, Young made his home there. In his diary he wrote, "March 1799: I finish plastering all houses and have whitewashed the fences around the animal pens. It is as in Wales."

Some twenty years later, however, in 1821, the Russian explorer Otto von Kotzebue found the residence in decline. "We now saw Young's settlement of several houses built of white stone, after the European fashion, surrounded by palm and banana trees; the land has a barren appearance."

"Barren it is. It looks like Baja, Mexico!" I exclaimed on the day that Paulette and I parked by the side of the road and walked through the desert terrain.

This part of the island gets less than ten inches of rain a year. "It probably rains less in a year here than it does in Wales in a week," she said.

And all that was left of the house was rubble covered with corrugated iron and some lumber. "Wales, me arse!" I said in my best Welsh accent, as we looked at the foundation. It was a rock pile.

KAMEHAMEHA . I

Archaeologists from the University of Hawai'i had excavated there; white hairs, which they hoped might be John Young's, or that of a member of the royal family—perhaps even Kamehameha—were sent to the lab for DNA testing. Everyone waited in anticipation, but the bristles turned out to be from a pig. According to ancient custom, the highest *ali'i* were buried in secret caves in the hills. Some speculate the remains of Kamehameha, which have never been found, are in the Waipi'o Valley where many *ali'i* are buried. Others say the tomb lies in an underwater tunnel not far from his temple, six miles from our house.

In charge of the royal arsenal, John Young was also appointed governor of the island of Hawai'i and served as an advisor to Kamehameha I and II. Not only a friend, he became *'ohana* (family) by marrying the king's niece after his first wife died. One of his daughters, Pane Kekelaokalani, was the mother of Queen Emma Kaleleonālani, wife to Kamehameha IV. Young and four others are the only white men buried with the royal family in the Royal Mausoleum in Honolulu.

The following Thanksgiving, my Hawaiian-history education continued when my father and I hiked through paths in the lava fields to where the sailors of the *Fair American* are buried. A metal gate barred the entrance to the mouth of the cave, and I stared at the lock on the latch of the bars. "You wouldn't want to go in there, believe me," he said. "I know. I went in there once, back in 1978." Then he told me his story.

"There I was on all fours, bathed in perspiration, ten feet below the ground, spelunking thirty feet into that black lava tunnel." He jabbed a finger in the air, pointing in the direction of the mouth of the cave. I couldn't imagine my father, a novelist and a painter, spelunking.

"It was so narrow my shoulders brushed both sides. My knees were raw from the sharp stones, and I had to duck my head from the stalactites," he said. "I'd liked to have quit. No space to turn, I quite literally would have had to back out of the deal, but then the others would have regarded me with scorn." My father walked with a limp from a bullfight goring in Spain, where he had learned the art of tauromachy after working for the State Department during World War II. Leaning on his cane, he looked up at the milky-blue sky and continued. "So I kept crawling along after the beam of light in front of me. Just when I thought my claustrophobia couldn't stand a moment more, I saw the light rise up—my guide was standing up! We were in a tiny cavern, about twelve feet by ten—a cave, yes, but less frightening than that tunnel. We could see four skeletons. Their wrists and ankles had been bound, their bodies trussed, slung from wooden poles like pigs to the market. Fragments of red neckerchiefs, powdery with age, were around their necks. I picked up a slipper-like shoe and could make out a few letters. The hairs on my neck rose. I hadn't quite believed the story of the skeletons until I read the shoemaker's trademark: 'Boston.'"

"So that shoe would have been made about a dozen years after the Boston Tea Party," I said.

"That's right," my father said, not missing a beat with his story. "Also, there was a pipe, a tarnished silver watch, and two ancient lanterns in the back. That's all. And enough. I took some photos and then we left."

"Do you think we can get permission to go inside?" I asked.

"I heard that vandals stole the pipe, the watch, and other articles some years back/ Besides"—he shuddered, wiping the sweat off his brow with a red bandana—"quite frankly I don't advise it. I still have nightmares about that awful tunnel and its spooky inhabitants."

Intrigued, I wanted to find out more of Hawai'i's past.

Robby continued his family story for Paulette and me one evening over Chianti on the veranda of his house. "There was another interesting relative on my father's side from the time of the *Fair American*: Robert Boyd, my great-great-great-grandfather, a ship builder and carpenter whom Captain Vancouver once met. When Kamehameha ordered Boyd to make a loom, Isaac Davis said, 'Don't teach the Hawaiians the *haole* technology. They are very clever and then we'—meaning him and Boyd—'would be out of a job.'" He

reached over to a stack of books and pulled out a copy of *A Voyage Round the World from 1806 to 1812.*

"It's by this Scottish sailmaker, Archibald Campbell, who recuperated here after both his feet were badly amputated." Robby thumbed through the book. "Davis said, 'They will soon know more than ourselves.' *They* meaning the Hawaiians. Campbell eventually did construct a loom to make material for Kamehameha's ships, but the other castaways were not pleased and a Hawaiian assistant worked the pedals as the poor buggah had no feet."

Sitting on a chair in the living room, I skimmed through the book while Robby grilled a leg of lamb on the barbecue and Paulette "talked story" with the women who were making poke in the kitchen. I read that the crippled sailmaker spent the end of his life pushing himself about the streets of Edinburgh with a barrel organ, telling tales of the South Seas and selling copies of his incredible book.

"Who were the most important voyagers besides Cook?" I asked Robby, changing the subject.

"Well, Cook was definitely the most amazing explorer and thorough documenter." Robby paused for a moment, then said, "Hawaiian scholars don't think Captain Cook was the first European to happen upon our islands; we *know* he wasn't."

"What? Our good Captain Cook?"

Robby told us that by the time Cook arrived, the Hawaiians already had iron, with no means to produce it. Spanish and Dutch maps exist that suggest there were landings here more than 150 years before Cook.

"Have you ever read *Shōgun*?"

"Of course, James Clavell's novel about the English pilot who sails to Japan," I said.

Robby explained that it was loosely based on William Adams, who piloted a Dutch ship, the *Liefde*, and, according to his chronicles, passed by the Hawaiian Islands.

I borrowed several books and articles from Robby and learned that, indeed, this story does coincide with a report in 1823 by Reverend William Ellis, who took a trip around the Big Island and wrote, "They have three accounts of foreigners arriving at Hawai‘i before Captain Cook."

I found out that a man on O‘ahu, Captain Rick Rogers, a former airline pilot, was mounting his own treasure hunt aboard his navy launch, loaded with equipment. I telephoned Rogers, and he answered from his boat the *Pilialoha* in the Hale‘iwa Harbor. Rogers said, "It's a mystery, but we know that the Spanish[13] came here between 1565 and 1815 on their trade route between Mexico and the Philippines. Some nine ships were lost—two of them in Hawai‘i—and the people aboard merged with the islanders."

"Do you think you'll find a sunken galleon?" I asked.

Rogers said, "Somebody will. But no gentle lagoons here, like in the Caribbean. This dynamic ocean moves things around. Tsunami, earthquakes."

"Volcanic eruptions?" I said.

"Could be covered in lava," he said.

"Any gold down there?"

"Some, more likely silver. The Spanish brought it from Mexico to trade in Asia. With the currents, shipwrecks were inevitable."

---

13. *One of Cook's officers Lieutenant James King sums it up, "We are driven indeed . . . to a supposition of the shipwreck of some buccaneer, or Spanish ship, in the neighborhood of these islands."*

A few artifacts from pre-Cook ships are in the Bishop Museum, including a *kaʻai*, an old woven burial casket, which was always kept with the monarchs. Inside, there is an ancient piece of iron attached to wood in the form of a dagger and an eight-foot piece of flaxen sailcloth dating from the 1600s, found in Kona.

Even if Captain Cook was not the first European to land on these islands, he chronicled in detail Hawaiian life before the extreme influence of the outside world dramatically changed it.

I looked forward to seeing Rogers's expedition and wished him luck. He said, "It's driving me nuts. I know there's a shipwrecked Spanish galleon down there. The proof: when I find it."

CHAPTER THIRTEEN

Man's Best Archaeologist

We dipped a finger into pink poi, and took a pinch of baked dog.
—CHARLES WARREN STODDARD, *SOUTH-SEA IDYLS*, 1873

Ever since he'd been a toddler, Will had wanted a dog. At birthdays and Christmas, a dog was at the top of his list. On the mainland, we traveled a lot, so it was impractical. For years, the neighborhood dogs got extra pats and affection while we fended off our son's pleas; we were in dog denial. We deprived him of every boy's dream, owning man's best friend.

He would kneel and put his hands together and beg like Al Jolson, "Please, please, Daddy! Oh, Daddy, why can't I have a dog?" He even wrote me a letter pleading his case:

Dear Dad,

Can I please have a dog? I know what you are thinking. It's too much trouble, but just let me try. Do you remember when you had a dog? How soft and cuddly it was? I need a dog for the days that I am alone. I need someone to keep me company. I'll do my homework and brush my teeth. I'll do anything, even all my chores and eat yucky vegetables. I hope you come to the conclusion that I should have a dog.

Love, Will

At age twelve, Will didn't have friends yet in his new school, and his brother was at boarding school. I scanned *The Honolulu Advertiser* for a Labrador, beagle, or a Jack Russell terrier, even though anything with four legs and a tail would have suited him. Locally, there are usually just poi dogs—mutts—available, or so I thought. In the Yellow Pages, I found Alpha K-9 Kennels, outside of Hilo, and called them to find out about dog boarding for future summers.

"What kind of dog do you have?" asked the woman on the phone.

After I said that we didn't have one yet, she asked what I thought about German shepherds.

"Not my favorite." I refrained from mentioning that one had once sunk its incisors into my back, leaving two bloody purple holes requiring shots and stitches.

"A shame. A two-year-old female was returned recently and needs a good home," said the woman. "Not too big, not too furry. Already trained."

"A lazy Lab is more for us," I said. But she was persistent.

"This one loves children. Almost like a Lab—the runt of the litter. East Berlin police dogs: her father is a Schutzhund III champion."

"Schutzhund?"

She explained that it was the German word for the sport of dogs. "We ship 'em worldwide."

That night, we stared at their website full of images of puppies and trained dogs for sale or stud service: the main feature—Omega von Young Haus, the father of the dog we were considering—was violently attacking a man's padded arms.

"Too extreme!" I exclaimed to Paulette.

"But on an island, you take what's available," she said.

A few days later, we drove through Waimea, past horse pastures and sheep farms, and through the old sugar mill town of Honoka'a, typical of the plantation villages that had existed throughout the islands before World War II. It looked like a cowboy town from a sepia-toned photograph. We went past three large gulches with grand waterfalls, up a country road, and through wild sugarcane, passing farms growing lettuce, papayas, and carrots, and turned into the driveway of Ted and Laurel Young's home. Dogs were barking as loudly as lions roaring in a zoo at feeding time.

As we stepped out of our truck, Laurel, a Hawaiian-Asian woman, greeted us, "Aloha! Welcome to the von Young Haus."

Ted Young, a tall, lanky Hawaiian, emerged from their ranch-style house. He told us that he had spent twelve years in the military training dogs, and during World War II, the German shepherds were used by both the Germans and the Americans. "The German shepherd was the official US Armed Forces dog," Ted said proudly to my wife, sons, and me, as we sat on a bench on the porch.

We expected to meet a Third Reich guard dog; instead, the sweetest animal with dark shadings timidly greeted each of us with an inquisitive wet nose. Will patted her head and rubbed her velvety ears, and as he smiled, the dog seemed to grin, revealing wolf-like teeth and a long tongue that dropped out.

Ted leashed and led the dog to his spacious lawn and demonstrated her obedience: When he stopped, she promptly sat. He slapped his left thigh, and she stayed behind him in a perfect heel. Ted put his palm flat to the dog's face and commanded, "Stay!" Then he walked all around the dog and out to the middle of the lawn. He motioned with his left arm, *"Hier!"* Some commands were in English, some in German.

My turn: Ted showed me how to lead the dog, and she followed. When the dog barked at Anthony, Laurel said, *"Phui"* (Shame), and the dog put its head down, aware it had done something wrong.

"Jedi's her name," Laurel said.

"Like *Star Wars*! Cool!" Will said.

Then Laurel showed us the documents of Jedi's impressive lineage. On the certified pedigree with the gold seal of the American Kennel Club were the names of Jedi von Young Haus's ancestors, including Prince von Haus Antwerp, Belgium; Uzone V. D. Wolfshohle, East Germany; Falko von Haus Freudlander, West Germany; and Lord von Friedeman Wolfgang, East Germany.

Champion pedigree puppies were $1,500, a trained dog $2,500. The price for Jedi, a little too small for breeding, was $1,800.

"I guess you guys are lucky I came along," I said. "I'd imagine most people in Hawai'i wouldn't pay that kind of money for *just* a dog."

"You know what?" Laurel said, "Even when they are poor, Hawaiians love their dogs and find the money for them."

As she put the crate in the back of our pickup truck, she uttered the prophetic words: "Don't lose that dog!"

On our way back to the west side of the island, Will said from the back seat, "Hey, Dad, can we put antlers on her next year and enter the Kona Christmas parade?"

That night, we put Jedi in her crate on the porch of the studio near the pond. I must not have secured both latches completely, because in the morning, Paulette shouted, "She's gone!"

I bicycled all over the neighborhood, shouting "*Hier*, Jedi, good, *gut ja*," in idiotic Pidgin German. But no luck. *Auf Wiedersehen* to my $1,800.

I searched for hours. Finally, I asked an old man who was taking his morning walk if he had seen a dog. The man, wearing gold-rimmed spectacles with a bookish mien, replied in a definitive Germanic lilt, "A lettle black sheep dowg, very frightened, ran zat vay and in za booch."

It was peculiar that something so special such as Schutzhund could be available on this outer island. Even more bizarre was to run into this man, so far from Germany, during his *sudsee* vacation, on the morning of losing our new German shepherd. Hawai'i is geographically the most remote place in the world, located in the middle of the Pacific Ocean, 2,400 miles from Los Angeles and 3,850 miles from Tokyo. The oddest things and the most unlikely people wash up on these shores. *Auwe!*

After another hour of searching through the brush in the lava fields, I saw a dark shadow move about a quarter of a mile away. She came to me, trembling and whimpering, as if wild boars had chased her. She wagged her tail between her legs.

"*Phui*," I said.

That was enough for her to know she should not escape (she never ran away again).

I became attached to that wolf-like sable bitch. She became a part of the family and helped make our little outpost more a home, less a vacation pad. When I'd come home at the end of the day, she would be waiting attentively in the driveway with her ears sticking straight up. Will would then tether her to a rope and the dog would tow him on his skateboard to the end of the road. I would bring her along on my evening walk on the beach, and she would wade through tide pools.

During dinner, Jedi would curl up on the front porch. When I'd come out, she would roll on her back and put her paws in the air and beg for a belly scratch with a peculiar whine, which effectively said, "Love me, love me!"

One day Bob Powers came over to repair the carport roof. Jedi ran to him, so I asked him if he had a dog of his own.

"Nope," he replied. "I took the advice of my father, who said, 'Son, don't bring home anything that eats and shits.'" He spat a wad of chewing tobacco on Jedi's back.

"Good luck to spit on a new dog," he said. Jedi wagged her tail, not seeming to mind a bit.

"Great guard dog," I said.

"That dog?" Powers said, holding back a laugh. "Scared of its own shadow." He waved his hand and she ran away, tail between her legs, and hid underneath the house.

Even though Jedi was pedigreed, she was still just a dog. And with hours and hours on their paws, free to lie about and run around, young dogs inevitably get into mischief, as we soon found out.

One evening we had guests over for drinks and *pupus*. These hors d'oeuvres are a custom in Hawai'i, and so is the removal of shoes before entering a house. Our guests left their shoes on the front porch, and while we were on the back porch—enjoying the view of Mauna Kea covered in snow, eating marlin poke and slivers of taro root, and sipping local white wine from the slopes of Mauna Loa—Jedi stole them.

We searched all over with flashlights. Eventually, Paulette gave the guests rubber sandals to walk home in. The next day, I searched under the house, where I discovered a labyrinth that resembled an archaeological dig site. Evidently, our dog had been busy digging holes. I never found the guests' shoes, but I did find several things that revealed the history of the house.

Jedi had unearthed a chipped porcelain teacup with "Matsonia" written on it: a relic of the long-gone Matson Line, from the great cruising days of the 1950s—an era of luxury travel when most arrived in Hawai'i by ship, including my family when I was a youngster.

Jedi also liked to jump in the pond. Out of the mud banks, she once dragged ashore half of a deep-sea fishing reel. It was corroded, but its handle was still intact. It looked to be from the fifties, from the time Puako was subdivided into 160 parcels: *Mauka* (mountainside) lots sold at auction for five hundred dollars while *makai* (seaside) ones went for eight hundred, the only stipulation being that you had to build. Purchasers from Hilo and Honolulu made fishing shacks for weekend beach retreats.

Jedi habitually drank the water in the pond, which worried me, as some of the freshwater streams and ponds have been known to carry Leptospira. There are one hundred to two hundred cases of leptospirosis annually in the United States; half are in Hawai'i. Rats are the primary culprits in spreading the bacteria, and there was no shortage of them by our pond. I had read in *West Hawaii Today* that a college student, visiting his family, had contracted leptospirosis while swimming in the Waipi'o River. Back on the mainland a week later, he went to an emergency room with a fever and other flu-like symptoms. In another week he was dead.

A train had once run through our backyard, I discovered, when Jedi unearthed yet another twentieth-century artifact: a railroad spike. According to history books, a narrow-gauge train, aptly named *Puako*, ran supplies to the sugarcane fields and brought the stalks back to the mill between 1902 and 1913. The locomotive was sold to the Dillingham Quarry on Oʻahu, where it hauled rock until a collapsed bridge stranded it. Rust never sleeps in Pouhala, Oʻahu, where *Puako* lies covered in vines. That rusty spike was a reminder of the little train that once chugged through our backyard.

Although Hawaiians have grown sugarcane in modest quantities for hundreds of years, it was not until the late nineteenth century that Americans and Europeans joined them, making commercial enterprises of sugarcane throughout the islands. In 1895, John Hind found some fine wild stalks of sugarcane in Puako. He traded a piece of land in Hilo with the Parker Ranch for Puako and added a plant, dormitories for three hundred workers, a company store, and two schoolhouses. A wharf was built, and a captain with an unquenchable thirst for rum ferried the processed sugar to freighters aboard a little tugboat named *Puako Steamer*. Floods, high winds, and drought forced the mill's closure in 1913.

Jedi also dug up a round, smooth rock that might have been used in ancient times for pounding taro into poi, or coconut bark into kapa cloth. There are more interesting archaeological sites two miles north, where there are some minor *heiaus*—stone religious platforms—and about two miles south of us, where there is an abundance of petroglyphs.

While walking Jedi along the little coral seaside trail one afternoon, Will and I found several small petroglyphs carved into the lava rocks. Most were primitive etchings of solitary stick figures; others appeared to depict whole families. We also came across many *puka*, holes about an inch in diameter and a couple of inches deep where ancient Hawaiians placed *piko*, newborn babies' umbilical cords. The mysterious carvings were scattered here and there in places where minor settlements had stood long ago, and near the beach, where ancient mariners had dry-docked their canoes. Scientists estimate that the petroglyphs were made about AD 500, and that the stone carvings were believed to be a form of communication between human beings and spirits or gods.

Excited, we headed inland with Jedi to the Puako Petroglyph Archaeological Preserve. A plaque marked its semihidden entrance path. Emerging from the kiawe forest, we came across smooth pahoehoe[14] lava rocks. Here was an oval-shaped area, 150 feet long by 60 feet wide, where thousands of designs were etched in stone: the Polynesian version of France's Lascaux caves. The only people there, we felt the thrill of discovery, as if we were the first to stumble upon this archaeological site. We found more of the strange stick figures—canoe paddlers, a fisherman with a pole and fish, and a chief with 209 marchers in a row. There are some three thousand turtles, fish, and canoes etched into the volcanic rock, and after seeing them, I was at a loss for words.

The petroglyphs raise more questions than answers about ancient Polynesia. They stand as evidence of a succession of life along this coast, parts of it still wild, which has hosted such a variety of souls over the last 1,500 years, and where each wave of settlers left traces of its passage. As I mused on what *we* might leave behind, Will pointed at the ground and said, "Whoa, Dad! Look at the big poop Jedi just made!"

---

14. *There are many different classifications of lava. The pahoehoe is hard, smooth, and sometimes ropy. The a'a is like a crunchy, loose rock.*

CHAPTER FOURTEEN

Bright Lights and Tiny Bubbles: Playing Tourist in Honolulu

So here's to the golden moon
And here's to the silver sea
And mostly here's a toast
To you and me.
—LEON POBER, "TINY BUBBLES," 1966

Longing for hip restaurants and shows, we hopped on the forty-minute flight to Honolulu, an Americanized city with Asian flair and nearly a million people, including visitors. As Paris no longer belongs to the French, so too Honolulu has its own international vibe belonging to the world; however, a certain Hawaiian style and rhythm seems to permeate everything—*mana*—emitting from the place itself and passed down through generations.

We checked into the Halekulani, meaning "House Befitting Heaven," where my maternal grandparents had spent winter seasons in one of the cottages during the 1920s.

My grandfather, once the captain of his school's swim team, told me about his memorable swims amid the Waikīkī breakers with the amicable Duke Kahanamoku and others of the Hui Nalu, a renowned surfing and swimming club.

Today, three high-rise towers have replaced the quaint old cottages. The Japanese-owned five-star hotel provides all luxuries, including a traditional afternoon tea served in the old part of the hotel. All

that remains of the original are some lava rocks from the foundation and a couple of old wood beams.

At House Without a Key, the seaside restaurant, we listened to the band play some of the finest island music and watched a former Miss Hawai'i move her lovely hula hands and sway her hips under the giant kiawe by the shore. Behind the musicians, surfers and canoe paddlers glided on the waves in silhouette as the sun's orange globe sank into the sea.

Earl Derr Biggers reputedly conceived his first Charlie Chan mystery, *The House Without a Key*, while staying in a cottage nearby in the 1920s. It's based on the murder of a former sea captain at that exact spot. The real-life inspiration for Biggers's legendary protagonist was Chang Apana, a Honolulu police officer—formerly a *paniolo* from the Big Island's Parker Ranch—who carried a bullwhip on the streets of Honolulu. Apana became a local hero, and through the Charlie Chan character his legend lives on.

The Halekulani is well known for making the best mai tai in the islands, so we ordered a couple. The late restaurateur Victor Bergeron once said, "Anyone who says I didn't invent the mai tai is a dirty stinker." Indeed, Trader Vic is credited with bringing the mai tai to the Western world, but South Seas islanders have been drinking mai tai–like concoctions for years. Nobody ever bothered to coin the word or write it down until 1944, when the trader mixed it up and served it to some visiting friends from Tahiti, who declared it *mai tai*, "good." The name stuck. Tahitians typically drank rum punch. Their version of a mai tai is basically a couple of fingers of dark rum and light rum, lime juice, ice, some water or fruit juice, and a couple teaspoons of sugar thrown in. Add wedges of pineapple or a slice of lemon, or whatever is on hand, until it tastes *mmmmai tai*.

Trader Vic's mai tai recipe is more refined:

MAI TAI

1/2 ounce orange curaçao
1/2 ounce orgeat syrup (almond syrup)
2 ounces freshly squeezed lime juice
1 ounce dark rum
1 ounce golden rum
1/4 ounce rock candy syrup
Dash of Angostura bitters

To garnish:
Sprig of mint
Maraschino cherry
Pineapple wedge
1/4 lime wedge

Fill a double lowball glass with crushed ice and add liquid ingredients. Cover with cocktail shaker and shake. Garnish.

The Halekulani mai tai differs slightly: a sliced stick of sugarcane is added, the fresh island pineapple is juicier, and a splash of light rum and an orchid top the concoction.

So-called Polynesian drinks were mostly invented by escapists during the "Tiki Pop" culture of the 1950s and 1960s. The first faux-Polynesian movement, however, began after the Panama-Pacific International Exposition in San Francisco in 1915. Americans were mesmerized by the hula dancing at the fair by the Bay. A vogue of Hawaiian-style guitar and ukulele music then raged throughout the United States and England. In 1916, the Victor Record Company, which evolved into RCA Victor, sold more records of Hawaiian

music than of any other genre. Years later, Bing Crosby crooned "Sweet Leilani" on his first gold record.

After the repeal of Prohibition, two Californians at opposite ends of the state funneled the faux-Polynesian craze, later dubbed Tiki Pop, to mainstream America. When Ernest Beaumont-Gantt put up palm trees at his roadside Hollywood café, Don the Beachcomber, it became a film industry watering hole with hula girl waitresses and a jungle decor. Gantt changed his name to Donn Beach and franchised his trademark from Chicago to Hawai'i.

Victor Bergeron followed suit with carved tiki, real shrunken heads, and black-velvet paintings of island maidens by Edgar Leeteg, the father of modern velvet paintings. He changed Hinky Dink's into Trader Vic's and, in 1951, opened a fancier version in San Francisco. It would be the headquarters for what grew into a global franchise.

After World War II, soldiers returned from the Pacific with tales of blue lagoons and tropical islands where women wore only grass skirts. Soon, Middle America was hearing the siren call of "Bali Hai" from Rodgers and Hammerstein's musical *South Pacific*, loosely based on Navy veteran James Michener's 1946 bestseller. Tiki Pop was further fueled by Thor Heyerdahl's 1948 adventure story, *Kon-Tiki*, and Michener's 1959 epic, *Hawaii* (the same year statehood was granted). Elvis Presley "rock a hulaed" with *Blue Hawaii* in 1961. Then *Hawaii Five-O* flickered on television, integrating the state into American cultural consciousness. Summer in the suburbs, from Chevy Chase, Maryland, to Pasadena, California, meant weekend luau parties complete with tiki torches and the whir of electric blenders whipping up frozen concoctions. In the modern decor of suburbia, it became fashionably bohemian to display primitive Polynesian art. Carved statues were set up near patio barbecues or out on front lawns across America, with few realizing that they were in fact displaying fertility symbols. As evidence, just look at some tiki—they're often well endowed. In the Austral Islands, *tiki roa*, the long figure, became the nickname for penis, and *tiki poto*, the short figure, was the designation for clitoris.

The word *tiki* has many meanings in ancient Polynesian. Tiki was considered to be the first man, a sort of Maori Adam who eventually evolved into a demigod. It is also a term referring to the carving of statues.

By the late seventies, however, tiki fashion was fading. As the public developed a more health-conscious attitude, deep-fried *pupus* were pooh-poohed, and lethal rum drinks were out. In the 1990s, the famed Trader Vic's headquarters in San Francisco closed down. The locus of paradise switched longitudes, from "Bali Hai" to Margaritaville, about the time Jimmy Buffett's songs became popular.

However, today tiki culture is reviving, with themed nightclubs opening across the world.

So, there we were at the Halekulani, sipping those famous tiki drinks and listening to genuine Hawaiian music as the Pacific washed the beach away and brought it back again. Was this a false paradise? Like most large cities, Honolulu has its share of crime and incivility—but not to the extent of similar-sized cities elsewhere. With the music, the smell of gardenias, the refreshing sea breeze in the mild evening, and the amber current of three rums flowing in my veins, I felt a magic in the air. To keep the glow going, I ordered a blue Hawaiian:

3 ounces pineapple juice
1/4 ounce blue curaçao
1 ounce golden rum
1 ounce cream of coconut

Mix in shaker with ice, pour into highball glass, and garnish with a lime wedge.

Harry K. Yee, head bartender at the Hilton Hawaiian Village in Waikīkī for over thirty years, knew what tourists wanted when he invented the most requested drink in Hawai'i, whose blue curaçao resembles the water of the lagoons. At first he used sugarcane sticks as a garnish. "People would chew on them and then put them in the ashtrays. When the ashes and cane came together, it made a real mess." He switched to orchids.

After our drinks, we slipped out of the elegant hotel and walked a few blocks past Don Ho Street to Kalakaua—the main drag—and into the Beachcomber Hotel's theater for the Don Ho Show.

As Wayne Newton is to Vegas, Don Ho is to Hawai'i. By the theater door, in a large rattan chair, sat the guru of "Rock-a-Hula." Don exuded the warmth of Hawaiian *ohana*. He shook hands with each guest and with genuine interest asked, "Where you from?" Paulette told Don that she was from Tahiti; he gave her an extra hug and exclaimed, "My cousin!" (They probably are; five generations ago, the first Chinese came to Hawai'i and Tahiti to work the fields and then married into Polynesian families.)

In 1980, I used to walk by the Don Ho Show and listen in from the outside. Back then, the thirty-dollar ticket was the equivalent of many meals on my student/surfer budget. Of course, those were the days in the islands when I was young and poor but very happy. Twenty-five years later, I was inside having my picture taken shaking Don Ho's hand. The crooner asked me what song I wanted to hear. "'Hua Li'i,'" I said—"Tiny Bubbles" in Hawaiian.

Don obliged, starting the show with *"Ti-ny bub-bles in the wine, make me hap-py . . .* You know, ladies and gentlemen, I hate that song. You would too if you had to play it every night for forty years. Nowadays, I play it first—in case I don't make it through the end of the show. Getting old, you know." He told many other jokes in his deadpan Pidgin style, including one about President Clinton's affair with Monica and how he could've saved the country sixty million dollars if he had just lived in Hawai'i. "Back in old Hawai'i, the king could have many wives, take all the women he wanted," Don said. "And most of us Hawaiians have intermarried so much we have some royal blood in us. They call me the King of Waikīkī; so, I can choose any woman in the audience, maybe even another man's wife. Hey, I bet some of you guys out there would be happy with that. Don't get me wrong," he continued, "I'm not running for office. Just think if I *were* president, they'd call me President Ho Ho Ho. Den they have to call the White House da Ho House."

Between jokes, the King of Waikīkī sang his signature songs, including "My Little Grass Shack," "One Paddle, Two Paddles," and "Pearly Shells," which he had us all sing along with him. The poetic Hawaiian language rolled off his tongue like waves lapping the shores of Waikīkī, and he made it sound simple to sing "the *humuhumunukunukuapua'a*[15] go swimming by." (*Triggerfish* is so much easier to say.) He gave the last *nukuapua'a* a deep rumbling mumble in the style of Elvis. The King of Waikīkī actually once played with the King of Rock and Roll, and performed with countless stars including Bob Hope, Burt Bacharach, Frank Sinatra, and Dean Martin. Like Martin, Ho had a thirst for social libations and liked to have a few drinks with the audience. His sets became parties, and people felt they were part of the gig.

Suddenly, the white telephone on the table by his side rang.

"Hello? Oh, Elvis!" He paused. "Yah, everything is fine up here. How is everything going down there?"

Don asked the audience, "Any Pearl Harbor survivors?" Five veterans stood up. "Great to have you here. God bless you," he said, and there was a round of applause. Don, a true patriot and former Air Force pilot, always played the National Anthem during his show. To background music, Don shared stories of the old days. "As a kid I used to dive for coins when the ships came in, so I could buy a can of food; otherwise, it was just fish and poi, you know," he said. "I eat lots of poi; it's all that keeps me stuck together. If you put poi on your face, sit in the sun, then pull it off, you look like Michael Jackson."

---

15. *Humuhumunukunukuapua'a is the state fish of Hawai'i. The translation is "triggerfish with the snout like a pig." Their skins appear to lack scales and have the colors of futurist paintings. Try saying it: "oohmoo oohmoo newkoo newkoo ah pooh ah ah."*

Just as the show started to seem like a routine of gags, Don introduced one of his ten children, Hoku. She energetically rocked and rolled, singing "Suck 'em up, suck 'em up time." (Most of the audience had quizzical looks on their faces, as they didn't realize that *suck 'em up* in Hawai'i is not a nymphomaniac's mantra but simply means "cheers" and is frequently heard at cocktail hour and last call.) A *hapa*, Hoku had blonde hair and island eyes, and was a fine singer.

The affable Don knew everybody. He had so much *mana* and charisma that people first became his friend and then a fan. On the way out, as he autographed our photo taken with him earlier, we discovered that we both had known James Michener, who was a good friend of my father. (He even spent a weekend at our house; his autographed books inspired me to travel to the South Pacific.) Don introduced us to his star hula dancer, Haumea Hebenstreit, who is the granddaughter of Robert Dean Frisbie, the poetic South Seas writer. Michener had raised funds for Frisbie's children, including Haumea's mother, nicknamed "Whiskey Johnny," to come to Hawai'i for their education. Haumea spoke with a crisp New Zealander's accent, about which Don kidded, "Sounds pretty, but we don't understand a word she says."

Before leaving, he asked Paulette to kiss him once more, which to my surprise (she's ordinarily very reserved) she did enthusiastically and said, "Aloha, Uncle Don." (In Hawai'i everyone fondly calls each other uncle or auntie or cousin or bruddah or sistah.) A standard part of Don's show is to invite the women in the audience, including the old grandmas, to line up and kiss him. Once, a granny's dentures came out and were stuck on Don's mouth. Another died in his arms. Don later wrote in his autobiography, "I swear, she was the most beautiful grandma I ever kissed, ever held in my arms. So I gave her one of my real suck 'em up kisses. Afterward, I felt this jerk against my chest." Don stopped kissing grandmas for a long time after that.

At seventy-four, Don's effervescent voice hadn't gone flat and his charm overflowed. Every night dozens of women would kiss him; the beautiful South Pacific hula girls swaying their hips by his side seemed to inspire him, like a kinetic Viagra. In 2006 Don and Haumea got married. He died of heart failure at seventy-six, on April 14, 2007.

After a few days of sightseeing and enjoying the bright lights of the city, we longed to get back to our island. Our bags didn't make the flight, so we waited for them at the Kona airport. We watched pale, jet-lagged mainlanders arrive, and, seeing them lumber around the baggage claim, my eyes caught Paulette's and we laughed. We felt we had become natives.

An hour later, we threw our bags into the back of our truck, which was parked under a sea grape tree, and drove up the coast in the fading light, careful of donkeys crossing the road. Like rubes after a fun weekend in the city, we were happy to head back to the old farm, or in this case, the *hale*. We jubilantly sang, "Pearly shells from the ocean, shining in the sun," and then "Hanalei, Hanalei moon." As we neared home, we fell silent.

That evening, I sat on the front porch and strummed my guitar, singing one of the ten songs in my repertoire:

Tiny bubbles make me warm all over,
With a feelin' that I'm gonna love you
Till the end of time.
Hua li'i i ka waina au hau'oli . . .

It was enough for the night.

CHAPTER FIFTEEN

Big Stars

But, as it still does today, Hawaii held another carrot for the rich and famous. In the islands, people generally leave them alone—no screaming crowds, no shouting paparazzi.

—EDDIE SHERMAN, *FRANK, SAMMY, MARLON & ME*, 2006

"You know who da guy I see?" Lalamilo said.

"Who?" I said.

"I wen' lawn moh-ah da Fairways, I see da Sundance Kid! I tip my hat *paniolo* style. Sez to da guy, 'Howdy, Sundance.'"

"You sure?" I reminded him, "You know, all *haole* look alike."

"I Ie da guy, yah. I know cause he look jus like in da movie, yah. You know dat part, he and Butch jump off da cliff and he yell, 'Shee—it,'" Lalamilo said.

Later that day, I heard, via the "coconut radio"—the gossip grapevine—that it was true. The wife of a friend of mine was working out at the Hapuna Beach gym when she spotted a face that looked like Robert Redford's, but he seemed much shorter. Indeed, it was the acclaimed star of celluloid. One of Redford's friends in the wine business lends him his place at the Mauna Kea Fairways whenever he wants to get away from Hollywood or to thaw out from the snow of Sundance.

My friend's wife hid behind a StairMaster and called her aunt, describing "Bobby" in every detail—including the amount of sweat soaking his T-shirt.

Earl Bakken, the inventor of the pacemaker and a founder of Medtronic—one of the largest hospital suppliers in the world—lives nearby at Kiholo Bay. In his thirty-thousand-square-foot beach house, run by a staff of eighteen, the elderly doctor enjoys the good life in one of the most beautiful parts of Hawai'i. Bakken has generously donated millions of dollars' worth of diagnostic equipment for CAT scans and MRI tests to the North Hawaii Community Hospital, though there is a shortage of doctors to work the machines. For the most serious operations, many residents fly to Honolulu.

One day, shopping in Kona, I saw Jesse Colin Young of the Youngbloods, famous for the sixties song "Get Together." The singer-songwriter started a 100 percent organic coffee farm in the hills of Kona, where all the coffee is handpicked—no machines. One morning after a cup of his Morning Sun, I found myself singing, "C'mon people now, smile on your brother . . ."

Many musicians have had places in the islands for years. When you live on an island and there is a big-name entertainer coming to town, it becomes the most important date on the calendar. At the Parker Ranch Rodeo Arena, Willie Nelson gave a whopping performance of all of his signature songs, from "On the Road Again" to "Mammas Don't Let Your Babies Grow Up to Be Cowboys." The country-western star flew over from his place in Maui with a few

young locals for his backup band. There was even a rumor that Kris Kristofferson might show up and pick his guitar, but he remained at his hideout in Hana.

While watering the front garden one afternoon, I swear I saw Clint Eastwood drive by in a classic convertible. But Paulette said, "It's Neil Young."

A couple days later, while picking up Will from high school by the tennis pavilion, I looked up at that same face and said, "Neil?"

"Who's Neil? And who are you?"

With a closer look, I realized that it *was* Clint Eastwood. I remembered Will saying that Eastwood's daughter was in his class. He squinted and looked like he was going to spit like Josey Wales. "Pardon, I'm just another parent," I said. Then he smiled.

My friend Robby Robertson invited me over to drink beers and watch the sunset from a house near his, which he caretakes. "It's the Youngs' house," he said. I didn't realize that he meant Neil Young until I saw him, with his mop of hair and lamb-chop sideburns, amble up the path with a golf bag and duck into his garage. As the sun set over the tops of the waves lapping the shore, Robby said, "He used to own land down by you, but it wasn't private enough for him, so he bought this old place on the point. Turned it into a paradise."

On one weekend jaunt to Waikīkī, after swimming in the lagoon, I ran into Mr. Margaritaville himself, Jimmy Buffett. The cheeseburger was in paradise—well, not exactly paradise. But the oasis-like atmosphere of the exclusive Outrigger Canoe Club might seem like it, amid the urban sprawl. Over the years, Buffett has put on many performances in Hawai'i and invites onstage with him local musicians like Henry Kapono and Jake Shimabukuro, the ukulele virtuoso. We chatted at the oceanfront bar, and I mentioned that

I'd been to Pitcairn Island, the home of the *Bounty* mutineers, where I'd heard his ancestors had once lived.

Jimmy tipped down his pilot's glasses and in a southern accent said, "I am a descendant of John Buffett, a sailor who was ship-wrecked twice and then, in 1823, decided to settle on Pitcairn as a schoolteacher."

"Did your family stay on Pitcairn?" I asked.

"No. Norfolk Island. They relocated many years ago," said Jimmy.

We talked for a few minutes, but then the musician/author/restaurant mogul[16] snapped out of the relaxed club mood and drawled, "Gotta go. Flyin' back to Flar-dah for a few days. Then sailing a cat in Bora Bora—bone fishing—and doing a gig at Bloody Mary's. See y'all in a couple of months."

On another weekend, we went to the Bruno Mars concert at the Blaisdell Arena. For a predominately young crowd, Hawaiʻi's prodigy, who once was billed as "the World's Youngest Elvis," crooned like Frank Sinatra, strutted like Michael Jackson, strummed his guitar and swung his hips like Elvis, and banged on the drums like Mick Fleetwood (the English drummer is retired on Maui).

Amid smoke bombs and visual-techno projections, Bruno played even better than he did at the Super Bowl halftime. The crowd sang along with him on "Just the Way You Are," but Paulette and I didn't know the words or any of this young-generation star's tunes. Just as we were feeling too old for the scene, we saw an elderly fellow in a tweed jacket walk through the crowd and to the back of the stage. It was Tom Moffatt, the show's producer and the original promoter of the famous Elvis concert in 1973 in the exact same spot.

---

16. *In 2009, Buffett, who once performed with Don Ho, opened a Margaritaville restaurant/nightclub in the Beachcomber Hotel, in the former location of the Don Ho Show. It closed just a few years later.*

Celebrities come to Hawai'i for the usual reasons—the warm climate and beautiful scenery, the friendly atmosphere, and the privacy. In Hawai'i, locals leave the famous alone so they can relax and be themselves. Charles Lindbergh lived on Maui and is buried there. Doris Duke, the tobacco heiress, lived on O'ahu; one can visit Shangri La, her house near Diamond Head, now a museum with the largest collection of Islamic art in the West. And, of course, a string of writers from Melville to Michener have passed through. Paul Theroux, author of fifty books including *The Great Railway Bazaar*, *The Mosquito Coast*, and *The Happy Isles of Oceania: Paddling the Pacific*, lives on O'ahu. A friend from my art class gave him a copy of my book, *Fabled Isles*. In his kind thank-you letter, he wrote, "I spend half the year here, and will be leaving at the end of May to head for Cape Cod, but in the meantime if you're near the North Shore, by all means pay me a visit."

Only in Hawai'i would the greatest travel writer of today hang loose and share the *aloha* spirit.

Many successful businessmen, mainly from the West Coast, also have homes here. At the end of our road is the hideaway of George Zimmer.[17] One day, while retrieving letters from my mailbox, I flagged down George as he rode by on a Balinese bicycle in a cloud of *paka* smoke. I told him that the best raincoat I've ever owned is from his Men's Wearhouse store and has lasted over ten years. He smiled and replied, "I guaranteed it, didn't I?"

Truth be said, the trench coat hangs handsomely unused in my closet; it hardly ever rains here.

While Anthony was on winter vacation, he introduced me to some kid from his boarding school who happened to be surfing at the

17. *In 2015, Zimmer bought Neil Young's place for twenty-two million dollars. Neil went to Topanga Canyon with Daryl Hannah.*

break near our house. "And this is his dad, Rob," Anthony said with a wink, while sitting on his board. As we shook hands, I recognized Rob Lowe even though he was in white face, covered in zinc oxide for sun protection—a good idea as he surfs almost every day near his house in Santa Barbara, where his son is on the school surf team. I couldn't help thinking of the scene where he wears a kimono, playing a Hollywood international negotiator for big tobacco advertising in *Thank You for Smoking*. I told him I knew Christopher Buckley, author of the novel on which that film was based.

"I used to be a photographer," I said, "and took some pictures for *ForbesLife* magazine. It's an editor."

"As a matter of fact," Rob said, "you might say I added to the story. It was *my* idea to have them smoking in outer space, and I insisted that it be in the movie. Do you live here full-time?"

"Yep," I replied. "Writing a book about Hawai'i—its history, et cetera, nothing too exciting compared to *Smoking*."

"Writing has been one of the most fulfilling things I have done," Rob said. (His autobiography is quite good.)

After two hours of many waves, he said, "I'm going in, gotta catch a flight in the middle of the night out of Kona."

"But there are no flights in the middle of the night."

"A friend of mine gave me a lift on his jet," he said sheepishly. "Just spent five days in Kaua'i surfing with Laird Hamilton." (Laird is the most famous big-wave rider in the world.)

"Wow," I said. But I was more impressed to meet someone—and a star—out of one of those private jets I spot regularly flying in like UFOs. At the Kona airport, I like to count how many sleek jets are lined up on the runway to whisk the rich and famous in and out. That's how I gauge the economy: thirty or more, bullish; only about five, bearish.

Another neighbor, one of the original venture capitalists behind Yahoo, throws an annual luau for two hundred of his closest friends and neighbors. A friend of ours wrangled us onto the guest list. As we filled our bellies with fresh fish, poi, and kalua pork, Eddie Kamae, a living treasure of Hawai'i, led the band. Kamae is like the Woody Guthrie of island folk music, with a hint of Django Reinhardt's jazz picking jingle to his ukulele, a style he has refined since the 1940s. With his group the Sons of Hawai'i, he influenced the 1960s revival known as the Hawaiian Renaissance. Many of his lyrics, often from ancient lore, derive from the Waipi'o Valley, where his father was raised.

When Eddie got to the microphone to say aloha, he spoke in the soft, reverential style the Hawaiians call *nahenahe*. He wasn't about to raise his voice over a luau-crazed bunch, half of them *haole*. From the island's soul, passed down through many generations, he sang about the love of the land and the people. His ukulele was tuned in such a way that when he played certain chords, it seemed to echo the ocean waves crashing on the wall just beyond the crowded lawn. Everyone fell silent and listened. He sang in *palupalu* style, his lilting voice like the lap of the surf. The island speaks to Eddie, and Eddie sings its message to us, and we can feel the reverberation of the ukulele—the essence of the island's *mana*—working its way into his music.

We were mesmerized. When the song ended many of us shouted, *"Hana hou, hana hou!"* (Again, again!) And he played more melodies after dinner. I whispered to Paulette, "This is the *real* thing."

"Not exactly Ala Moana shopping center music," she said.

The technology-money crowd is flocking to Hawai'i and developing it. Bill Gates owns a large property past Anaeho'omalu Bay, and Michael Dell, owner of the Kona Village Resort, has a stunningly expensive house some fifteen miles down the coast. In 2012, Larry Ellison bought 98 percent of the island Lāna'i (minus the three thousand inhabitants) for six hundred million dollars from Castle & Cooke, which had acquired it with its takeover of Dole Pineapple. Islanders wonder if the chief of Oracle will become the chief of paradise and build another authentic Japanese palace like his two-hundred-million-dollar home, or do like most developers and just pave it over.

The inventor of Viagra has a place by Kohala Ranch, and one of the founding investors of Intel has a home nearby.

Then there are the more modest folks, such as my accountant, who, after tax season, relaxes at his condo by the Mauna Lani golf course. Our house looks like a shack compared to his luxurious place, but of course ours *is* just a shack, with remodeled additions spanning some fifty years.

So many successful people, seeking to escape modern life, are buying and building in Hawai'i that it may end up becoming what they were trying to escape. As malls sprout in Kona, traffic jams worsen. Joni Mitchell's prophetic lyrics to "Big Yellow Taxi" come to mind:

> *Don't it always seem to go*
> *That you don't know what you've got*
> *Till it's gone?*
> *They paved paradise*
> *And put up a parking lot.*

CHAPTER SIXTEEN

Cockroached Gasoline

The sea rang its monotonous changes—fair weather and foul, days like death itself, followed by days full of the revelations of new life . . .
—CHARLES WARREN STODDARD, *SOUTH-SEA IDYLS*, 1873

Fishing is a sport where men go out early in the morning and return late with the smell of beer on their breaths and a peculiar need to exaggerate the size of their catch. But in Hawai'i, the fish really *are* big.

One afternoon, I took my twenty-four-foot fishing boat, the *Wahanui* (Big Mouth), fifteen miles up the coast from Puako with my friend Mario. Mario had been a boatswain and a charter captain, but he sold his boat to become a fine woodworker. When he built the cabinets in our kitchen, all we talked about was fishing, and there is nothing more fortunate for a boat owner than to have a friend who is a professional guide, content to fish for fun.

The *Wahanui* was my fourth boat over the past twenty years. Experienced at deep-sea fishing, but for a different kind of fish—salmon on the West Coast of America—I was finding the technique of Hawaiian-style fishing for ono, ahi, mahi-mahi, and marlin to be a whole different game. We trolled at a speed of twelve knots (instead of two for salmon fishing) in a mesmerized trance, as if resigned to a long voyage, zooming through the water and watching the plugs bob in our wake. We were a few miles past Red Hill with four lines out. Two green-and-blue lures pulled on the inside, and "pink ladies" swung from the twelve-foot outriggers. Spinner dolphins (a hundred of them) leaped, spun, and dived around the boat, smart enough not to strike the lures, before they swam farther out to sea.

An albatross scythed along the combers, circling our boat. The largest of all seabirds, the albatross has a wingspan of up to eleven and a half feet and is burdened with superstition. For hundreds of years, sailors have regarded it with awe, and some even believe albatrosses are the reincarnated souls of evil sea captains. At times, they are viewed as good omens, and at others, bad. Through its long hooked beak, this one screeched and uttered unearthly cries, as if in distress.

A fish struck the outside lure. The rubber band snapped on the outrigger as the line dropped taut, catching the hapless albatross across the neck and taking him underwater. By the way the line screamed off the reel, I knew it was a good-sized fish. I grabbed the rod and began to retrieve the line by reeling and pumping. Just when I had half the line back in, the fish dived again. Pull and reel, once more. Finally, the fish neared the boat and we could see that it was a big tuna, but tangled in the line was that great bird, now lifeless. According to the US Fish and Wildlife Service, a hundred thousand of these endangered birds perish from unfortunate encounters with fishing gear every year.

"Meu Deus!" cried Mario. They were probably the only Portuguese words he knew, passed down from his grandfather who had come to Hilo to work the sugarcane fields. He quickly crossed himself and then kissed the little gold cross hanging from his neck.

I pulled in the line; Mario gaffed the tuna expertly behind the gill plate, yanked it up onto the deck, and whacked it on the head with a bat. Then, regarding the poor bird, lying limply on the deck of the boat, he broke into verse: "'And I had done a hellish thing,/ And it would work 'em woe:/ For all averred, I had killed the bird/ That made the breeze to blow.'"

Mario, who always had a cigarette dangling from his lips or a beer at hand when out fishing, had written his senior paper on "The Rime of the Ancient Mariner" because he loved the sea. Occasionally, when he was sufficiently oiled, he would recite verses from Coleridge's epic poem in perfect English. He never seemed drunk as he expertly tended the lines and watched for signs of fish, but he was always in a fairly constant state of lubrication, alternately chuckling at his jokes or cussing if things didn't go smoothly. On this day, he had been giving mouth-to-mouth resuscitation to many bottles of beer over several hours.

We untangled the line from the bird's neck and, miraculously, it gasped for air and coughed up water. It shook its wet feathered head and struggled to its webbed spatula-like feet, dazed and standing unsteadily. Amazingly, the bird had survived a one-hundred-foot dive underwater. Majestic as it had been while soaring in the air, on deck it now lurched pathetically up to the bow, where it rested vacantly.

Then the engine gave a sputter and went silent. I could hear the screech of terns, the swishing breeze, the flicking sound of flying fish jumping from wave to wave and, a loud burp. Mario. He then broke into another verse from the only poem he knew: "'We stuck, nor breath nor motion;/ As idle as a painted ship/ Upon a painted ocean.'"

"Coleridge was cool, da kine, yah?" he added.

"Garans," I replied, using the Pidgin word for guaranteed.

He took another swig of his beer and ad-libbed, "Water, water everywhere, and got plenny beer fo' drink."

Looking at me, he said, "Whatsamatta? You, babooze—start 'em up, brah."

I turned the key. Nothing. When Mario realized that I hadn't cut the engine, he jumped out of his chair and his beer-fueled poetic trance.

"Check the oil," he said, in full command.

We looked down below at the oil tank. Okay. Mario then turned the key. "More of nothing," he said.

After five minutes of troubleshooting, he figured something was wrong with the fuel line. And yet another problem was brewing—a strong wind was pushing us out into the 'Alenuihāhā Channel, which essentially flows out to the open ocean. In that narrow funnel between the Big Island and Maui, the trade winds blow hard. "If we get pushed out there, it'll be 'ha-ha' to our asses," Mario said.

The albatross, still standing on the front deck, spread its wings into the strong breeze and was airborne with one flap. Albatrosses exploit the wind and can glide up to one hundred miles without flapping their wings. They can speed up to eighty miles per hour and travel five hundred miles a day. Some circumnavigate the globe; the typical fifty-year-old albatross has flown over 3.7 million miles.

"Start the kicker," said Mario.

I lowered the fifteen-horse Honda, pushed the red starter button, and pointed us toward shore. But after twenty minutes, we were losing power.

I squeezed the rubber ball on the gas line, and the engine sputtered back to life. When I had bought the engine, the salesman said that it could run "forever" on just a teaspoon of gasoline. Five more minutes were all we needed.

Mario stood on the bow, anchor and rope in hand, directing me to steer toward the shallow of the cove. He threw out the anchor and yelled, "Cut the engine!"

I didn't lift a finger; it just sputtered to silence. Once anchored, Mario said, "Someone cock-a-roached da gas."

Impossible, I thought. We had filled the tank to the top during the previous trip. But we had been off island on our summer vacation, so someone could have siphoned off the gas.

"Dat, or somet'ing blocking da fuel line," Mario said.

We hoisted up a red life preserver on one of the outriggers. A boat was motoring a mile away from us. As it approached, we frantically waved the life preservers and sounded the horn. The boat passed us by. "I can't believe they didn't see us," said Mario.

We stayed in the calm of the cove, which had a depth of about twenty feet. A gust of wind howled and moved the boat, which tugged on the anchor rope. "We're dragging!" I yelled, hoping I didn't sound too frantic. We let out more line, hoping the anchor would snag on a coral head. I stared at it bouncing off the ocean floor, and from the bow I saw the reef drop off to forty feet of water and then a little farther, an abyss of blue.

Just as we reached the end of the rope, the anchor stuck.

"Get ready to jump," said Mario.

"Jump?"

Looking at the current pulling out to the wide-open ocean, I didn't want to be bobbing shark bait.

"Swept out to sea with this wind. There's nobody out here to get us."

"What about the Coast Guard?" I naively asked.

"They're all the way over in Hilo. It'll take 'em eight to ten hours to get us, and by then we'll be thirty miles out to sea, with just beer and that *pilau* tuna—no way, brah," he said, shaking his head emphatically.

The choice was to jump overboard and swim to the safety of the nearby shore or stay with the boat and endure a long parched voyage. Insurance came to my mind. Jump, yes! I happily visualized a Lloyd's check for forty thousand dollars. Mario called his wife on

his cell phone and told her to four-wheel it down and meet us on shore. I went below and put my wallet in a plastic bag.

The anchor held on the last coral head before the blue water, and from just north of the point, a boat's red Bimini top appeared. "With this weather, that'll be the last boat." We waved the life jackets vigorously, but it kept going. The plight of castaways. At the last minute, someone apparently glanced our way and recognized our predicament, and the boat turned toward us.

The power catamaran, with the words *Aquatic Research Vessel* stenciled on its side, pulled alongside us. The state-owned vessel operated by the University of Hawai'i to study the fish population and habitat had seven divers aboard. A curvaceous bikini-clad student threw us a line. We hauled up the *Wahanui*'s anchor, and soon we were being towed at nine knots, decent trolling speed. "Don't let them see us doing this," Mario hissed in a vesper whisper.

We dropped a couple of lines over the side and turned the swivel seats astern to watch the lures bob up and down. Without our engine running, it was almost as quiet as sailing. To celebrate our rescue, we popped open cold beers and ate our sea rations—a turkey sandwich and an apple. The reel started to scream, and Mario quickly turned off the clicker, reeled a few times, and handed the rod to me. "All yours," he said.

Pull up and reel, again and again, until a silvery-green, blue-and-yellow-finned jack trevally came alongside. "Just an *ulua*," said Mario as he reached down, grabbed the leader, slipped out the hook, and released the fish. Some of the coastal fish, including the Trevallys, have ciguatera poisoning, caused by toxins in the coral.

Once inside the Kawaihae Harbor, the dive boat set us free. We thanked them as the *Wahanui* glided to the finger dock. We secured the lines and winched it up on the trailer. Then we drove to the gas station. Surprise: the tank was six gallons short of full. "The gas wasn't cock-a-roached after all," said Mario. "But somet'ing *lolo* about dis boat, brah."

I hoped that breaking down at sea was the end of my bad luck with the boat. But soon the depth finder expired. Then the battery went *pau*. Next, the manufacturer recalled the engine. Finally, the warranty ran out. Oh, sure, we had caught a few fish and enough excitement to keep us going out again. Like the time we had a double hookup with a pair of thirty-pound mahi-mahi, and another when we caught a forty-pound ono, which made for weeks of onolicious dinners. Or the day we caught a couple of small aku tuna, five-pounders, which we then live-bait rigged for marlin, but no hookup. By the time we got to shore, after ten hours of fishing, we were hot and exhausted, so we settled for a sashimi dinner of the bait!

It's hard to find these fish in the windy wide-open ocean, so Mario suggested that we fish off Kona, which he knew like the back of his hand. "We have to haul the boat down there anyway to get the engine fixed," he said. "And I need to catch a grander," he confessed with fervor.

Five years earlier, Mario had caught a 980-pound blue marlin. One big fish, but not enough to put Mario on the exclusive list of two thousand fishermen across the world that have caught a marlin over one thousand pounds. For a professional like Mario, an *almost* grander didn't measure up. So we set about planning an expedition to the Honokohau Harbor, Kona, home of the Hawaiian International Billfish Tournament. I was thrilled that Mario still wanted to fish with me after our fiasco with that boat, and that we were setting out to catch a trophy—a lifetime feat.

CHAPTER SEVENTEEN

Hemingway and Fishing with Christie Brinkley

Uliuli kai holo ka mano. Where the sea is dark, sharks swim. (Sharks are found in the deep sea. Also applied to men out seeking the society of the opposite sex.)
—MARY KAWENA PUKUI, *'OLELO NO'EAU: HAWAIIAN PROVERBS & POETICAL SAYINGS*, 1983

The night before the Kona expedition, Paulette and I went to Lulu's, Kona's hot nightspot. It was packed with revelers, both locals and tourists of all kinds. On the bar was a plaque inscribed "Hemingway pissed here." As I had spent two years writing a book titled *Hemingway's France: Images of the Lost Generation*, I was happy to get away from *anything* to do with the writer. Yet, it turns out that Hemingway most likely did piss there. In 1941, while on his honeymoon in Honolulu with his third wife, Martha Gellhorn, he was summoned over to Kona to verify what was believed to be a world-record black marlin at 815 pounds and thirteen feet in length.

Hemingway found that the Kona skipper Charlie Finlayson had cleverly invented a fighting chair that could have changed the sport, but after Hemingway's insulting letter to the International Game Fish Association, the contraption fizzled into fishing history. "The Clapp catch used a fishing chair built something like a rowing seat. The rod butt was in a socket, which was a part of the chair. The rod and reel were attached to the chair, the back of which would be rolled back and forth by the attendant. Being attached to the chair, the pull of the fish would pull the chair and the rod forward. The guard or attendant would then pull the back of the chair back, thus gaining line on the fish, which the angler would only need to recover by turning the handle of the reel." Hemingway concluded that the seat unfairly advantaged the angler, Charles Clapp, and couldn't be considered legal for the IGFA: "The entire fishing device was designed to make it possible for anglers who had never fished before to catch big fish without being subjected to any strain on any part of their bodies except their reeling hand."

Hemingway, always in the limelight of the world, then disappeared for a few days. He went up the slopes of Mauna Kea.

In Waimea, just a couple of weeks before our night at Lulu's, Harry Wishard, a talented artist of island scenes, had handed me a black-and-white photo of the famous author standing beside a man on horseback with a bighorn sheep slung over the saddle. "My grandfather Leslie Wishard let the Hemingways stay in his guest cottage for a few days, and he arranged for the *paniolo* to guide him hunting," Harry said. "The *paniolo* assured Hemingway that all the way up Mauna Kea, they had very fine wine."

"Yes," I said. "He liked fine wine and preferred Margauxs and Bandols."

Harry said with a sly smile, "But when it came time to serve the wine, after the arduous journey, guess what? Screw-on-cap sherry. When those *paniolo* of 'O'okala came into town, all they bought was rice and bottles of cheap sherry."

"Pretty simple living up there then?" I asked.

"Yah, sheep, sherry, and rice," Harry said. He knows the territory and is an expert hiker and hunter in the outback of Hawai'i.

From Kona the Hemingways returned to Honolulu, finishing their trip at the Halekulani Hotel. Martha wanted a honeymoon and wrote about the islands, "This is a place where hospitality is a curse and no one can be alone." Their belated honeymoon had gotten off on the wrong foot, right from the beginning, when they had stepped off the SS *Matsonia* in Honolulu and were adorned with no less than eighteen leis around their necks. Martha later wrote in

Travels with Myself and Another that Ernest said, "I never had no filthy Christed flowers around my neck before and the next son of a bitch who touches me I am going to cool him and what a dung heap we came to and by Christ if anybody else says aloha to me I am going to spit back in his mouth." (Their marriage didn't last long.)

Before departing for Manila, Hemingway prophetically stated, "Japan will attempt to tie us up in the Pacific." It was only ten months later that the Japanese imperial forces bombed Pearl Harbor.

Like Hemingway, I had become an aficionado of deep-sea fishing, and the Kona coast is ideal for it. The morning after partying by the plaque at Lulu's, I was steering the *Wahanui* through the Honokohau Harbor. Mario was fiddling with the tackle, and along the sides of the canal, people in wide-brimmed hats fished with long poles for mullet, mackerel, and other pan-sized fish. Waves were breaking on either side of the channel entrance, and we idled in the clear turquoise water inside the break wall. After a set of south swells passed, I nosed the boat out while Mario squared the deck. Soon we were skipping over the water like the flying fish leaping beside us. Just a few hundred yards offshore, there is a bountiful reef—a haven for billfish, tuna, and wahoo. When we reached the deep ultramarine-blue ocean, Mario threw out the lines.

A course was set, and there was little to do except talk story. With a cigarette dangling from his lips, Mario cracked open a couple of beers, turned the passenger seat backward, facing the lines, and sat down. I thought of the line from John Williamson, the lieutenant on Captain Cook's voyage who wrote, "A Seaman in general would as soon part with his life, as his Grog."

Between swigs, Mario spoke of his sport charter days. His favorite client had been Christie Brinkley, the supermodel and ex-wife of Billy Joel. "What did she wear?" I asked.

He paused and gazed out to sea with longing adoration, as if he were envisioning a goddess. "*Auwe!* I was tending the lines, and she come out da cabin wearing a white see-through shirt, a pink bra, and white shorts. Da kine short shorts." He took another sip of his beer and reminisced as if it were yesterday, even though over fifteen years had passed. "Den she wen' go fore-deck fo' sun tan. Take off dose short shorts and shirt and all she have is one itsy-bitsy, tiny-weenie pink bikini."

"Was anyone else on the charter?"

"Well, der was one husband. No remember much of him, 'cept dat I t'ought 'bout push 'm over da side, den stay forever fish wit da kine." Mario took another drag off his cigarette and looked back at the fishing lines wistfully.

Contemplating the clouds on the horizon, he searched for diving seabirds, which would indicate where the baitfish were. As there were no working birds at that moment, he talked story about taking a group of "Japanee" businessmen and one of their daughters out on a fishing charter. His mate knew a little Japanese from a couple of classes, but the rest he had learned from porno movies, and he frequently mixed up the pronunciations. The mate tried to say, "I like fishing with your family," but instead it came out "I'd like to fuck your daughter."

"The father of the young woman was the head of a large corporation . . . Mitsubishi, Sapporo, all same," Mario said. The men had laughed in embarrassment. Thinking he had a hit, Mario's mate repeated the phrase several times. The Japanese went below and remained there until there was a fish on. Mario was dismayed that they didn't leave a tip. Only later, once the mate mastered the language after many classes, did he learn the actual meaning of his words. The following year, the same girl was back in Kona, enamored with the idea of living the island lifestyle. The mate invited her for sushi. They hit it off and eventually got married. "Only in Hawai'i!" I said to Mario, and we laughed until we were interrupted by the scream of the reel. Mario grabbed the rod and lifted it over his shoulders, then leaned back and set the hook. The fish was pulling so hard that he put the rod back in the gunwale. I strapped on the harness. Once the line slowed down, I clipped the harness to the reel and placed the butt of the rod in the cup of the waist holder. The rod bent in a pulsing rhythm, and I felt the weight in my belly, arms, and shoulders. Mario pulled the throttles in reverse, and waves slopped over the transom, drenching me, but what did I care—I was hooked into the fish of a lifetime. White beads of water ran along the line, taut as a steel guitar string. The fish dived deep, stripping out most of the line. I could feel the force of the beast's power; it felt as if I were fighting an amphibious mustang.

Then it stopped diving. It ascended. I reeled in the line like crazy. A long-beaked shape leaped across the water like a water-skier jumping the wake. Marlin! After skittering across the surface in a series of half jumps, it landed, sending an enormous column of white spray into the air. "A blue!" shouted Mario.

It dived again, taking most of the line. For an hour, I wrestled the fish until my arms ached with fatigue. Finally, that magnificent creature came alongside the boat, its sides streaked with silver, lavender, and blue; pectoral fins spread wide; and that scythe-like tail moving side to side. Mario grabbed the cable leader with one gloved hand and pulled the fish closer. With a swift jerk, he stuck the gaff into its neck. The fish thrashed and thumped the side of the boat. Mario next sank a large hand hook in its back. "Tie dis to da cleat," he yelled. I wrapped the white rope around the cleat. With the gaff in his left hand, he held the struggling fish tight to the boat. Then—*thwack, thwack*—he smashed the blue head with a silvery steel bat. It went still. I grabbed the tail, and Mario lifted the front portion over the side of the boat; it landed on deck with a thud and lay there gasping. At that moment, it wasn't just a fish but a colorful being of the sea, a strange visitor from another world. It flopped violently, and its swordlike bill stabbed at the air. I thought of the Kona fisherman whose eye had been poked out by a marlin after it jumped into the boat. Mario handed me the club. I struck it twice. Blood splattered on my legs and arms, and the white deck of the boat went crimson. Then the marlin died. Exhilarated by the struggle, we hooted with joy and shook hands. Mission accomplished!

After hosing off the deck, Mario covered the fish with a wet canvas tarp. A shrouded corpse. I peeled it back for another look: blood trickled from its mouth. I touched its flesh, cold. Emptiness and a certain sadness overwhelmed me. I had never felt that way about a fish before—definitely not about an ono, with its teeth snapping, or even a glittering salmon destined for our dinner table. Just a few minutes earlier, that marlin had been a beautiful living animal, swimming fast and free with its blue, green, black, and white colors ever changing in the light of the bright sun. Now it was a man-sized cadaver, and I the murderer. Every fisherman has a heart, and mine was heavy at that moment.

Back at the dock, the fish weighed in at 180 pounds. Far from a grander, but great Kona fishing.

A week after I sold the boat, Mario stopped by the house. He cracked open a beer, and we sat in fishing chairs on the porch over the pond and fed breadcrumbs to the tilapia. In a moment of weakness,

I admitted that I missed the *Wahanui*. Mario said, "You know what kine boat's mo' bettah?"

I've loved to talk about boats ever since I was a kid and read up on all the different models in yachting magazines. I brightened at the prospect of another tale. "Whaler? Tiara? Azimut?" I said.

"Nope," Mario said. He took a sip of beer, shook his head, and stared out across the pond. "Odda people's boat."

CHAPTER EIGHTEEN

Hurricanes and Tsunami

In the midst of a tropical revolving storm, one contends not only with huge waves and winds of a hundred miles an hour and more, but with a considerable rise in the level of the sea itself, caused by the sharp drop in atmospheric pressure.
—NORDHOFF AND HALL, *THE HURRICANE*, 1936

In all, the state of Hawai'i includes 137 islands stretching thousands of miles from the eight main islands, pointing like the bones of a hand toward Japan. Starting with the island of Hawai'i, they string out 1,500 miles to the lagoon of Kure Atoll, the world's northernmost coral atoll.

One Saturday, a little after eight, Paulette and I were sitting on the back porch after a sumptuous meal, talking story and staring at the stars—another typical tropical night—when the porch suddenly shook and rocked back and forth, settling into loose soil. There had been high tides lately, and I thought that surely the foundations had precipitously fallen into the mud. On the ten o'clock news, we learned that a 5.0 magnitude earthquake had occurred. I'd experienced the 1989 earthquake in San Francisco and still remembered the panes of glass falling from downtown buildings and the flames of the Marina District's fires. I had hoped to escape earthquakes, but it turned out that seismic jolts are common in the islands.

The following morning, the volcano Kilauea blew, spewing out red-hot lava and sulfurous fumes. The day after that, it was announced that a hurricane would strike at 5:00 a.m.

I was putting away a ladder when Lalamilo pulled up in his old truck, on his way to secure one of the big houses down the street.

"*Pele* is *kolohe* to da max. Squeeze *'okole*. Secure everyt'ing *wiki-wiki* or it fly like *manu*." He waved his arms in the air like a bird, and then sped down the road. It was the only time I had ever seen him in a hurry.

We put away gardening tools, bicycles, surfboards, and all small patio furniture. We brought out water bottles, put fresh batteries in the flashlights, and battened down the hatches.

The air was warm and still. When the first winds blew, they were sickly, hot, and heavy with moisture. Every hour, we watched an update on television as the hurricane steadily approached, until the power went out. A lukewarm tropical deluge fell in biblical torrents. The wind howled and moaned, then it whistled like steam from an infernal locomotive. The trees creaked, limbs blasted bare of leaves. Branches cracked and heavily thunked to the ground. The roof shuddered, and I feared it might blow off like many did when Hurricane Iniki devastated Kaua'i in 1992. That last major tropical cyclone had winds at 227 miles per hour, clocked by the navy.

After a restless night, we were relieved to learn that the hurricane had veered 150 miles south of us. Our yard was a mess, but we still had a roof over our heads.

Every winter, torrential deluges cause flash floods. On one such occasion, it had rained only a few hours before I headed out to pick Will up from soccer practice. I passed a particularly low stretch of Puako Beach Road where muddy water was flowing briskly, put the truck in four-wheel low, and enjoyed the nearly amphibious ride across the torrent. Once I was above the Queen Ka'ahumanu Highway, the storm clouds cleared, and the scenery of the high country flanking the road changed to green volcanic hills. The rocks and the dirt along the sides of the road were a reddish brown. The pavement meandered up the slopes, past a green sign with white letters: "Welcome to the Parker Ranch."

In 1815, John Palmer Parker, who first came to the island for the sandalwood trade, was hired by Kamehameha I to shoot some of the marauding feral cattle. Parker selected the finest animals as payment, starting his own herd. Then he married Kamehameha's granddaughter, who inherited 640 acres, and bought an additional 1,000 acres. This was the beginning of what would become one of the largest privately owned cattle ranches in the United States, totaling 225,000 acres, or 9 percent of the island of Hawai'i.

In the town of Waimea, I picked up my son from school and headed home. Down on the coast, ahead of us were flares and the blue flashing light of a police car. "Sorry, sir, the road's washed out." A few hapless motorists were stuck there. It looked like we might have to spend the night in the car, until the road would be cleared. Will was getting hungry and tired, so I backtracked a couple of miles to the deluxe Mauna Kea Beach Hotel and reserved a room. Soon we were dining in one of its candlelit restaurants, Will in his sweaty soccer jersey and I in my gardening garb, enjoying seafood soup and range-fed Parker Ranch steak, with sliced taro and fresh Waimea spinach. Living well is, indeed, the best revenge.

Will asked, "How did children get to school in the old days, before cars?"

"Donkeys." I knew the answer because I had recently read in *Paniolo House Stories* that the children rode donkeys from Puako, past the Wailea, Hapuna, and Kauna'oa (Mauna Kea) beaches, to Kawaihae. As Katy Wishard Lowrey told it, there would be "two or three of them on a donkey and their dogs following and older children walking alongside the donkey."

"This sure beats walking or riding a donkey," Will said, through a mouthful of mud pie.

On the way back to our room, we marveled at the Asian and Oceanic art adorning the hotel, built in the 1960s by David Rockefeller. Ghoulish idols of New Guinea and statues of Buddha seemed to ogle at us around every corner.

I remembered spending a vacation there with my mother, who was an architect, loved Hawai'i, and danced the hula. Even when riddled with cancer, my mother was always ready for a tennis game on the resort's courts. Though it had been fifteen years since her death, I missed her terribly at that moment and wished my son could have known her.

In the morning, the view from our balcony embraced the cerulean sea and one of the loveliest beaches in the world. What a place to wake up in after a stormy night. I could bask in the caress of paradise for quite a while, but Will had to get to school on time. As we drove back up to Waimea, the heavy clouds were just lifting off the top of the Mauna Kea volcano, revealing a white blanket of snow. Poli'ahu, the ancient snow goddess who is believed to live on the mountaintop, had spread her cloak far down its slopes.

And then came the Big One: On Sunday morning, October 15, 2006, a 6.7 magnitude earthquake struck, its epicenter a mere six miles from our house. Roads, bridges, schools, and houses were severely damaged. Hospitals were evacuated. The top floor of the Mauna Kea's building collapsed, and the hotel closed.

We were in Honolulu that weekend and returned home to find our South Pacific painting collection hanging at odd angles above broken dishes and books scattered across the floor. Cracks ran up and down the sheet rock on the walls and ceiling. Some lava rocks had tumbled off the man-made waterfall. The carport sagged. But it was all minor damage and we were thankful; farther up the coast, some houses were completely lost.

A few weeks later, we drove down to Kailua-Kona and visited the Hulihe'e Palace, which managed to keep its first floor open for a while despite needing a million-dollar fix. Kahea Beckley, the stately palace tour leader and local historian, said, "You know why people from all over come here and build houses? Because it's the best place on earth. Cleanest ocean and climate." Then he added, "Why can't one of those babooze billionaires who build their fancy houses up the coast just make a big donation? Billy Gates, Mickey Dell, Chucky Schwab—it's nothing to them. But for us, our heritage, it's all we have." He threw his hands in the air, dramatically staring up at the pictures of the kings and queens of former years hanging from the cracked walls. Athough the museum is interesting, on that day, there was an acute sense of departed glory.

Kahea sighed. "But somehow, the Daughters of Hawai'i"—who run the palace—"will raise the money." Just then, two men from FEMA arrived to assess the damage.

One morning at five thirty, I awoke in the darkness to the ringing of the telephone. I hobbled downstairs thinking, *It's just another East Coast person who forgot we're six hours behind.* Instead, a friend from California said, "Tsunami is heading to Hawai'i. I saw it on the morning news."

Paulette got up and turned on the TV. "Go back to bed. It only hits the Hilo side," I said and crawled under the covers for a few minutes until the screeching tsunami-warning sirens pierced the stillness and forced me to get up and throw all essentials into a suitcase. With my laptop and all paperwork, I went back downstairs. The newscaster said it would be a couple of hours before the tidal waves would reach Kona.

After breakfast, as I loaded the car with survival gear—blankets, food, and water—a policeman drove down our little road shouting into a bullhorn, "Hawai'i Police Department: evacuate immediately!"

With my two best surfboards strapped on the top, we headed out of the driveway, taking one look back. This was it. Goodbye to our house. "Wait a minute," said Paulette, and she got out of the car and quickly picked a few flowers as a remembrance.

Once on higher ground, we parked by the Ka'ahumanu Highway, along with hundreds of other cars. We hiked up a small hill for a better view of the killer waves to come. With a 300 mm lens focused on the reef and the cover of *National Geographic* magazine in mind, we waited. Finally, the ocean receded and then surged back in, several times over a thirty-minute period. It was like watching a video in fast motion of a tidal change from an extreme low to a high.

The road to the coast remained closed, so we drove up three thousand feet to the town of Waimea and went to a friend's house to unwind for a couple of hours, but we ended up wired in front of the television. We learned that South American earthquakes had triggered the tsunami and that the phenomena's power is difficult to forecast. In Hilo the tidal surge was six feet, only half of what scientists had predicted. It could have been like the one in 1946, one hundred feet of water sweeping in and taking out half the waterfront and killing ninety-six people. Nearby, Laupahoehoe lost twenty-five, including sixteen school children and five of their teachers.

The next evening, while on the beach watching the sunset, we ran into our neighbor, Haunani Woods. She lived in a plantation shack with a corrugated-iron roof and a ramshackle sloping porch with a frangipani tree out front. "When I heard on the news that a tsunami might be on its way, I packed all night and left at four thirty in the morning to avoid people scrambling to higher ground, getting gas and food."

"Good idea," I said.

"It reminded me of the tsunami that hit my hometown, Hilo, in 1960. We had to cook our meals on kerosene stoves. Power station on the waterfront was wiped out. Sixty-one people were killed, and one was my friend."

"How old were you?" Paulette asked.

"We were only thirteen. It was heartbreaking to see her empty desk once school reopened," Haunani said.

"Very sad," Paulette said.

"Yes. But we are so lucky now that we have warning in advance. However, if the quake is close to us, there is no time." She went on to describe the one in 1975 that hit south of Kona, at the idyllic retreat Halape, killing Dr. Mitchell, whom everybody knew. A Boy Scout troop, Sierra Club members, and some fishermen—a total of thirty-four people—were camping over Thanksgiving weekend when the sea washed over them. Nineteen were injured and two died, as did four horses.

"Maybe next tsunami, we won't have time to pack," I said.

"That's right. A tsunami can travel five hundred miles per hour—fast as a jet! Most of them come from Asia or the Aleutians, but if closer?"

"Whew, exhale!" I said.

In March 2011, one year after our scare, a 9.0 earthquake off Japan triggered a massive tsunami, killing over fifteen thousand people and wiping out towns in the Land of the Rising Sun. We followed the same routine as before: we packed our survival gear, and at 3:15 a.m., we watched on television the tides rising at Waikīkī. Twenty minutes later, they would reach us, so we hopped in the car and drove to higher ground. This time the tidal shifts were more drastic; several buildings were damaged, including the Kona Village *hales*, and a house floated out in Cook's Bay. Once again, our beach shack was spared.

In October 2014, another hurricane entered our part of the world. Again, we got gas, food, and water and battened down the hatches. Luckily, it veered away in the final hours. Generally, the slightly cooler water of the Pacific Ocean causes wind sheer that diverts the hurricanes. Occasionally, they strike, but not as often as in the Caribbean.

CHAPTER NINETEEN

Canoe Paddling

E kāmau iho i ka hoe. (Keep paddling.)
—OLD HAWAIIAN SAYING

Ocean sports are woven into the fabric of life in Hawai'i, and outrigger canoe paddling has been number one for over 1,500 years, ever since the ancient Polynesian voyagers landed on these shores. There are clubs throughout the islands, where people of all ages paddle for fun or competition, and it is a way for Hawaiians to connect with their heritage. (In Honolulu, even the Elks Lodge, that venerable institution associated with Middle America, has its own canoe team as well as several sleek vessels.)

I decided to give paddling a whirl and drove to Tiger Canoe & Kayak in Kailua-Kona, where, inside a warehouse, masked men fine-tuned the carbon molds with sanding machines. Tiger Taylor, a fourth-generation Hawaiian of Portuguese descent, told me, "With the racing season coming up, I'll put you on the waiting list for the latest model."

While it was being built, I picked some *'ulu* (breadfruit) leaves off the small tree in our garden for a custom design on the bow and stern.

Months later, Tiger drove up to our house with the long, smooth white canoe strapped on the roof rack of his truck. I carried the *ama* (outrigger) and the *iako* (aluminum bars that fasten the *ama* to the *wa'a*, the canoe). Tiger put the canoe down gently on our back lawn, and while he assembled it, he admitted that he had sold only a few of these professional-style canoes to complete beginners. Most of his customers belonged to clubs and competed. He instructed me on the basics of how to paddle, and to climb aboard *when* I *capsize*.

I wanted a lightweight canoe—not to go fast, but to easily carry it to the beach anytime I fancied.

A mere eighteen pounds rested on my shoulder as I walked out the front gate and turned left at the street. Then I heard a sound—*dunk*

keechssshhhh. I looked back and saw that I had clipped the rock wall. It would take practice to negotiate corners with a twenty-four-foot craft on my shoulder.

With a little experience kayaking and paddling heavy wooden canoes, I placed mine in the water, hopped in, and stroked the paddle. On the second stroke, I felt a bump, heard a scratching sound, and looked down at a coral head. The rudder was nicked, but luckily not the hull, which Tiger had described as "fragile as an eggshell."

I waded out a little farther, hopped back in, and pulled the blade through the water. Across the shallow lagoon, I glided, steering around multicolored coral heads by pushing the pedals to the rudder and guiding the canoe through the blue pass in the reef. Skimming over the tops of the waves like a flying fish and speeding down the swells, I shouted, "Yahoo! This is easy!"

I shifted the paddle from the outrigger side to the open side. One stroke and a slight ripple caused my weight to tilt over just a bit. It took barely a second to *huli*, or flip over.

Hat and sunglasses gone—no problem, just reach down and pull on the leash. In my excitement, I'd forgotten to attach the Velcro ankle bracelet that was supposed to tether me to the canoe, which a gust of wind picked up and sent flying through the air like a twirling albatross. Flailing in the blue water a quarter of a mile offshore, I swam, paddle in hand, toward the canoe, but the wind was pushing it farther out to sea. Finally, I reached the *ama* side of the vessel and shakily hoisted myself aboard. I attached the leash, a lifeline I wouldn't forget again, and paddled toward the coast.

As my confidence returned, I looked around. I heard a slicing sound like tearing masking tape—flying fish jumped on both sides, skipping from wave to wave. Bright-colored fish swam below the surface. I realized that when canoe paddling, you don't merely float on the ocean, you feel as if you are a part of it, like a quiet water strider feeling the surge of the swell.

I entered Paniau Bay, which means "pulling water," so named for its strong currents. A few months earlier, I'd ridden my bicycle there after I'd heard ambulances, police cars, and a helicopter roar by my house, and watched a group of men haul a body onto the back of a pickup truck, drape a shroud over it, and bump along the coral path to an ambulance—another drowning victim. Reflecting on the fate of that man, I nervously turned the canoe around and paddled back up the coast.

The canoe started to shimmy. I looked down and saw the *iako* dangling from the *ama*, which was not parallel to the canoe but was *kapakahi*, askew. I must not have twisted tight the screw that attaches the stem to the outrigger. I leaned on the outrigger side of the wobbly vessel. Below me was a deep blue crevasse in the coral reef—a perfect spot for a tiger shark to hang out and snatch unwitting turtles and . . . In front of me rose a group of coral heads where waves crashed. I needed to fix the *ama* before hitting the reef.

I swung one leg over the canoe for stability. With the paddle, I pulled the outrigger back in, parallel with the canoe. I carefully inched closer to a calmer spot. Away from the beastly coral heads, I slipped overboard and into the water. Clinging to the vessel, I twisted the knob of the *iako*, securing it to the *ama*.

Safely back in the canoe, I paddled over the deep blue crevasse, out to sea, far from the breaking waves. Up the coast and through the pass, I glided over the shallow turquoise-green lagoon. Back on the white coral-strewn beach, I let out a sigh of relief. There was much to learn.

Eventually, I did get the hang of paddling, and every so often, I would steer between the rocks and coral heads of the shallow lagoon and venture into the ocean. On one excursion, I saw three humpback whales surface like submarines a mere hundred yards from me, spouting plumes of white spray into the air. "Thar she blows," I said, for no reason. Not wishing to get whacked by their massive tails, I paddled into a cove and waited for them to swim away.

Whenever I see these great creatures, I cannot help but think of the beginning of Herman Melville's *Moby Dick*: "Call me Ishmael. Some years ago—never mind how long precisely—having little or no money in my purse, and nothing particular to interest me on shore, I thought I would sail about a little and see the watery part of the world." Melville's writing, though part fact and part romantic fiction, was actually an excellent documentation of seafaring. Only two generations after he wrote *Moby Dick*, the greater tragedy was not the end of the *Pequod* and her crew and the white whale, but the end of a world in which such adventures were possible.

After waiting fifteen minutes, I hoped the whales had passed, and I nosed the canoe out of the sheltered bay and paddled up the coast. Suddenly another giant breached, its entire mass seeming to float in the air for a second before falling back into the sea. *Thah-wump* came the terrifying sound of thousands of pounds hitting the water. I steered closer to shore, but the waves were pounding the rocky coastline. Between the two perils, it was a narrow course back to the pass in the reef near our house.

For my afternoon read, I picked up the Bible (a rare occasion) and opened it to the first book of Genesis, where I found "And God created great whales." And they are great. And every year, they migrate from Alaska to Hawai'i to breed, returning again and again.

CHAPTER TWENTY

The World Series of Surfing

*Waves are not measured in feet and inches, they
are measured in increments of fear.*
—Buzzy Trent, big-wave rider, 1955

The powerful waves of the Banzai Pipeline have killed thirteen people. As with downhill ski racers and bronc riders, the element of danger is seductive, and every year for five weeks in November and December, professional surfers from Brazil, Europe, Japan, Tahiti, and practically everywhere there are waves, converge on Oʻahu's North Shore. The most consistent winners have been from Australia, Hawaiʻi, and California. They chase a million dollars in prize money and the glory of world titles in the Triple Crown. The real money is from company endorsements.

Seeing some guy "spit out the barrel"—ass backward with his legs in the air, like a circus performer of yesteryear being shot out of a cannon—sounded fantastic. So Paulette and I flew to Honolulu, rented a car, and drove north to Sunset Beach. There we met Randy Rarick, the executive director of the Triple Crown of Surfing, who was up on a ladder working on the scaffolding. Randy had won the State Surfing Championship in 1967, but by 1975, when the world tour was formed, he was too old to star, being all of twenty-six.

I told Randy that I had bought one of his boards back in the Lightning Bolt days; he was flattered. "It's now an antique," he said.

"I think *we're* antiques," I countered.

"Well, not really," said Randy, perhaps a little defensively. "Gerry Lopez is in his late sixties and was recently featured in a magazine riding a fifteen-foot wave on a stand-up."

"Mr. Pipeline himself—Arnold Schwarzenegger's sidekick in *Conan the Barbarian*?" I blurted.

"Yah. And Peter Cole is in his eighties, still here on the North Shore." Peter is one of the big-wave pioneers of the late fifties we see on old posters.

"That's great to hear," I said, as Randy lumbered down the ladder.

He pulled up a couple of chairs and told us about the new surf stars. "Kelly Slater, eleven-time world champ, is the Lance Armstrong of surfing. After Slater's seventh title, the cyclist even sent him a note welcoming him to 'the No. 7 Club.' About every generation, there is one surfer who comes along and revolutionizes the sport."

"Who's next?"

"There's always a faster draw that comes along. The major change in the surfing world is that girls are in a golden age—a natural evolution. Women want to be a part of surfing."

"It's amazing. They surf like . . . well, just like men," Paulette said. We had recently seen videos of the women surf stars in the biggest events, the Reef Hawaiian Pro Haleiwa and the Roxy Pro Sunset Beach.

The next morning, Paulette helped me spread out a towel on the sand at Sunset Beach, and we watched through binoculars the Roxy foxes brave the wicked west swell. A crowd was gathered near the judges' tower in the center of the beach as points were tallied based on style, maneuvers, and size of the waves. The emcee, a retired professional from the world circuit, announced, "And now, folks, we have a contestant dropping down the face of an incredible outside wave—ten feet high! A radical backside turn and . . . another."

All we could see was a tiny dot floating down a massive wall of water a half a mile out to sea; a white snail trail indicated the turns. The dark dot, which appeared the size of an ant on the mountain of water, went straight down and then back up, turning 180 degrees, no less than four times. Then other surfers were up on waves until the horn sounded, and another five women paddled out through the strong currents.

Women have surfed in Hawai'i since the days of Kamehameha. Princess Ka'iulani would surf in the waves of Waikīkī while Robert Louis Stevenson waited under a banyan tree, ready to towel off the lovely olive skin of the *hapa* lass. The intellectual half-Scottish, half-Hawaiian princess was Stevenson's muse; the world's best-selling poet of his day was smitten with the surfer princess. On the beach of Waikīkī, what a marvelous mermaid she must have seemed to the tubercular romantic.

In the islands, I had met Rell Sunn. She was a pleasure to talk to on the beach and always seemed to have a smile on her face, especially when she would hold her arms in the air as gracefully as a hula dancer as she arched her back in the curl of the wave—the

epitome of stylish surfing. This ballerina of the waves was known as the "Queen of Mākaha." When she got cancer and all her hair fell out, she continued to surf. Everyone watched the queen when she surfed. Even as her body withered away, she surfed until the end.

Over the next few days, we'd go down to Sunset, sit on the beach for a few hours, and watch all the surf stars ride those fearful waves. Carissa Moore, local girl and a world champion, really shone; however, the most impressive was Bethany Hamilton, who surfed big waves with just one arm!

The most unusual contestant was the prodigy John John Florence, age twenty-two. His first three waves were tube rides that buried him inside the curl of the wave. I had actually seen him win contests years ago at age fourteen, a skinny little kid about five feet tall, looking like he should be holding a scooter instead of a six-foot board. The surfing world is banking (he earns five million dollars per year) that this lad, who has surfed the Banzai Pipeline since he was eight years old, will be the top surfer for at least a decade.

We drove a few miles down to Laniakea, a renowned reefbreak with long waves. From a distance, it looked like good surfing for me, but there was a rip current pulling harder than a max ebb tide out the Golden Gate. Two lifeguard trucks were parked under a tree by the beach, and one lifeguard walked down and asked me, "If you lose your board, can you swim in?"

"I have before," I assured him. But I didn't say that it had been thirty years before.

As I waxed up my board, I reminisced about that earlier day at Laniakea: I had been a young surfer dreaming of being a professional, surfing neck and neck with Shaun Tomson. The son of a wealthy property owner from Durban, South Africa, Tomson was the Great Gatsby of surfing amid the raunchy Australians and the beach boys of Hawai'i. With twelve world-tour wins under his belt, and features in forty surf movies, Tomson also started the fashion line Gotcha; its success landed him in stylish Montecito, California.

That day at Laniakea, thirty years before, Shaun, known as one of the fastest paddlers of all time, turned and said, "Set, paddle," and took off. I followed as fast as my arms could pull me through the water, and we went up and over a series of waves. As I was scratching to get over a big one, Shaun just turned around and caught it. And then the most monstrous wave I could have imagined snatched the board from my arms. The leash ripped out the glassed-in plug, and I did my first long-distance open-ocean swim. When I picked up my board, the bottom was broken through in three places, though the topside had held together, with its fiberglass still intact. It folded like an accordion. I loved surfing, but at that moment I realized that my chance of making it into the elite pro circle was between slim and none. A few months later, I gave up my dingy apartment in Waikīkī and finally listened to my mother: "I wish you would graduate from college."

I did, and that was the end of a youthful illusion.

Paulette settled down on the towel and opened a book. A lifeguard picked up a board from the beach. "Tenth board broken today," he said.

With adrenaline already revving, I walked down to the water, attached the leash, paddled to the inside section, and caught a little wave. The rip pulled me back out as though I were a skier on the bunny slopes hanging on to a rope tow. Then I caught a massive wall, and it rekindled that thrill of big-wave riding. There is a line in *The Sun Also Rises*: "Nobody ever lives their life all the way up except bullfighters." *Surfers should be added to the list,* I thought afterward.

After surfing, we went to the North Shore Surf and Cultural Museum in Haleʻiwa and stared at photographs of the greats, from Duke Kahanamoku to contemporary surfers. Surfboards of all shapes and forms are stacked on the racks, displaying their evolution. Some were made of balsa wood; others were pre-1940s and carved from redwood. One had a glass box through the middle—good for watching the fish and spearing lunch. In the 1950s, surfers worked out of their garages to hand-shape styrofoam blanks that would be sealed with resin over sheets of fiberglass. Boards are still made this way, except technology has advanced with stronger yet lighter materials. The first surfboards were finless. A fin like a small keel was added, then another; today, boards have three or more.

A fascinating piece in the museum is a large red board with a motor in the middle—the first motorized rescue board, manufactured by Alfred Bloomingdale, the department store heir. Bloomingdale hired Fred Hemmings[18] to promote it, but on its 1965 debut, it stalled in front of the Royal Hawaiian Hotel and wouldn't restart. The prototype was the only one ever made, but after its motor was repaired, it went on to serve in many rescues. Today, lifeguards use jet skis to get out through the waves quickly and pull people to safety.

After the museum, we went to Ali'i Beach for another surf session. I paddled out to the lineup and recognized a surfer I had seen at the contest earlier that day. When I asked him if he had been at Sunset, his face lit up.

"Did ja see me? Der in da pocket of action."

"I sure did, along with a thousand other people."

"I bet on da beach dey say whodaguy? Yah."

A set rumbled and he exclaimed, "Pockets of action. Chance um, brah!" (Go for it, brother.)

The gigantic waves thundered in from the outside, and the group of us looked up at them like altar boys before God. I scrambled up a face along with the other fools, but I got pitched under. My leash stretched out into long linguini. Another liquid beast pulled me, and I felt as if I were being sucked over Yosemite's Vernal Fall. *Hammered.* I finally surfaced and gulped for air. Miraculously, my board popped up from a boil of water. To say the least, I was in over

---

18. *Fred Hemmings, 1968 world champion, was the founder of the Pipeline Masters and the International Professional Surfers world tour. He was a member of the Hawai'i House of Representatives from 1984 to 1990 and served as a Republican member of the Hawai'i Senate from 2001 until his retirement in 2011.*

my head. But as Eddie Aikau[19] once said, "You got to take a few in order to make a few." In other words, you have to eat it before you get the chance to ride the big ones.

A gray-haired Aussie paddled by on his way to easily pick up a few waves with dignity in the rough seas. He said, "A bit suss, eh? Breaking bigger than the day they held the Hawaiian Pro" (the first event of the Triple Crown, held at Hale'iwa).

Eventually, I caught a good one in. On shore, I inspected the damage to my new board. Handprint indentations marked the rails where I'd gripped for dear life. Dents dotted the deck, from elbows and knees smashing against it. My bruised left arm was turning yellow and green. *Well*, I thought, *I can still do everything as if I were twenty-five years old—except now it hurts.*

That night at dinner, back at the Turtle Bay Resort, I ran into the graying Australian whom I'd seen surfing. "Weren't you out today at Hale'iwa?" I asked.

"Yeah, mate," he replied with a grin.

It was Wayne "Rabbit" Bartholomew, world champion in 1978, whom I'd met more than twenty years before. Rabbit was the president of ASP (the Association of Surfing Professionals) and champion of the over-forty division of the Quicksilver Masters. Not to be confused with Rabbit Kekai, the classic Hawaiian surfer, Rabbit Bartholomew grew up poor in Queensland, lifting wallets on the Gold Coast. He went on to win many titles and was the first big showman—surfing nude for *Tracks* magazine, and appearing in *Surfer* wearing aviator glasses, a silk boxer's robe, and gloves like

---

19. *Eddie Aikau was a legendary lifeguard. When the Hōkūle'a broke apart in a terrible storm off Moloka'i in March 1978, he volunteered to paddle his surfboard to help. That was the last anybody saw of him. "The Eddie" surf contest is held at Waimea Bay, but only if the waves are over twenty-five feet!*

Muhammad Ali. He wrote an aggressive article, "Bustin' Down the Door," in 1976 for *Surfer*, a manifesto on competitive surfing that was interpreted by some Hawaiians as an insult; that year, on the North Shore, he had a front tooth knocked out. Within this competitive sport, some surfers resent outsiders, especially *haole*, coming to their spot.

With Paulette content to explore the spa at the Turtle Bay Resort, I went another day in search of surf. At 'Ehukai Beach, a mutual friend introduced me to the then-current world champion, Kelly Slater. I said, "I've moved to the Big Island. I'm just about at retirement age."

"Me too," Kelly said.

I laughed. He didn't. At age forty-one, he *was* at retirement age. Several of Kelly's friends have died in this perilous occupation. "See you on the golf course in about ten years," I replied. (Kelly is an avid golfer in his downtime and is a natural.)

He ran into the water and paddled out for a training session. His first wave was impressive, as he flew off the top, but I've seen others do it. I grabbed my board, and while stroking out to the lineup, we talked. I mentioned that we had something in common: we both grew up in Florida. (I had spent six years of my childhood in Kelly's home state.) "Well, you must have gotten good at fishing," he said. "Not much surf there."

There sure is surf here, I thought, and I was surfing with the best in the world, *el numero uno*. He paddled farther outside and caught a wave. Sitting on the inside, I had a perfect view of the champ as he approached the critical section. It looked like he wouldn't catch up with the curl, but, unpredictably, he flew off the crest, and in midair, like a helicopter, he twirled around 360 degrees. With his feet still planted on the board, he landed as easily as a dolphin and continued his next turn before disappearing in the tube. We've seen this on film, but in real life—unbelievable. The live view of an acrobat in flight, in my face, was better than a front-row seat at any event. Kelly's flexibility and love of surfing are what separate him from the pack. In the athletic world, someone like this is one in a million—Rocky Marciano, Babe Ruth, Mikhail Baryshnikov, et cetera.

A few days later, we went to the ultimate event in the Triple Crown—the Pipeline Masters. In the final heat was John John Florence, the rising star, and Kelly Slater, older and wiser, going mano a mano. We parked about a quarter mile away and walked down to where crowds were perched on beach towels right in front of the crashing waves. On the sand, we stood among bikini-clad beauties and bronzed titans of the sea and watched as John John caught a few impressive waves with instinct, at the spot where he grew up. When it came to be Kelly's turn, the wisened pro chose

a wave and disappeared into its pipe. It spit out water and foam—along with Kelly, gracefully standing with arms in the air in a sign of victory and thanks. But he was not unscathed; when he walked to the judges' stand to receive his trophy, he held his arm, which was possibly fractured. What a thrill it was to watch the sport evolve professionally and see the creation of legends before our eyes.

Not everyone appreciates the invasion of competitors, however. Later that afternoon, after watching the waves at the Pipeline, I was crossing the parking lot when up drove a rusty pickup truck with oversized tires. Hanging out the back were a pit bull and a mangy, mean-looking mutt, jumping up and down with their tongues drooping and drooling. A big Hawaiian got out, on his shirtless torso a mélange of badly executed tattoos. He softly chided his dogs, "No step on da boards." Then he turned to the massive sign with the names of previous winners, mostly Hawaiians and Australians, on the scaffolding of the Pipeline Masters competition. He raised his two closed fists in the air with the middle fingers extended and shouted, "Fuck da Triple Crown!" no less than three times. Then he got back in his truck, turned around, and laid some rubber on the asphalt.

CHAPTER TWENTY-ONE

Tough Guys Wear Skirts

They brandish'd Their Weapons, distort'd their Mouths, Lolling out their Tongues and Turn'd up the Whites of their Eyes Accompanied with a strong hoarse song, Calculated in my opinion to Chear Each Other and Intimidate their Enemies.

—LIEUTENANT JOHN GORE, *COOK'S VOYAGES*, 1769

Still on vacation on Oʻahu, Paulette and I drove past cow pastures, shrimp farms, and the old sugar mill of Kahuku, to the town of Laie,[20] home of the Polynesian Cultural Center. As corny as an amusement park full of islanders in ancient garb sounds, this enormous tourist attraction offers a splendid introduction to native culture, comprising the entire Polynesian Triangle—bound by Hawaiʻi, Easter Island, and New Zealand at the corners, with Tonga and Samoa on the west and Tahiti and the Marquesas in the middle.

---

20. *Laie is pronounced "Lie-yeh" by the chiefs and "La-e-ah" by the commoners. Take your pick; most people call it "Lie-yeh."*

At the center, we were warmly greeted by a group of Tongans dressed in grass skirts, feather headdresses, and shell beads. Visitors can try their hands at weaving Fijian baskets; swinging strings with balls at the end, Maori style; or squeezing coconut milk as Samoans do. The center also attracts its fair share of Elvis fans; there's an enduring rumor that Elvis lives there, in the guise of an overweight chief.

Elvis loved Hawai'i and built his second home here while filming *Blue Hawaii* and *Girls! Girls! Girls!* Much of *Paradise, Hawaiian Style* was filmed at the then-new cultural center, with its double-hulled outrigger canoes full of dancing and singing Polynesians. The

waterfalls that served as a backdrop still flow. His three Hawaiian movies introduced the songs "Return to Sender," "Can't Help Falling in Love," "Rock-A-Hula Baby," "Blue Hawaii," and Elvis's romantic rendition of "Ke Kali Nei Au," the Hawaiian wedding song, still among his most popular titles.

We could have floated through the canals in canoes, but chose to walk, and started with the Hawaiian village. There, outside a pandanus-leaf hut, a woman named Hina showed us how to play Hawaiian chess. We moved little pebbles across a flat lava rock with slight indentations carved into the stone, marking the spot for each piece. Of the thirty-six spaces, four were left empty. Hina, her long, thick black hair giving way to salt-and-pepper strands, said, "The game of *konane* is played similar to Chinese checkers. One can jump many times, as long as in a straight line—no diagonal and no L-shaped jumps. The last move wins. You can also win by blocking your opponent so they can't move a pebble." It was a relaxing, stress-free game, and we won. (I later concluded that Hina let us win just to see the joy on our faces.)

Paulette loves to watch dances and comedy skits, so I agreed to see several at the various villages, and we concurred: Our favorite was Aotearoa, the Maori name for New Zealand. In the middle of this village stood an A frame building decorated with intricate wooden carvings. Once inside, we took our seats and watched young men dressed as warriors gyrate and hula dance. I had learned in Hawai'i to never laugh at the big guys wearing dresses—they are the Samoans and Tongans—and not to snicker at the knickers of men with New Zealand accents wearing black-and-white beaded miniskirts—they are the Maoris. They performed the "ugly face" (or haka, as it is called in Maori*)*, once a war tactic used to psych out enemies. The men shook and slapped their tattooed bodies, stuck their tongues out from their tattooed faces, and grunted fiercely. The New Zealand national rugby team still performs the haka in front of its opponents before every match.

When Captain Cook, the first European to explore New Zealand, sailed around the island, he described the haka as "strange contorsions (sic)" and recounted that the Maori shouted at him and his men. He later learned the meaning of their words was "Come ashore with us and we will kill you with our patu-patus." The patu-patu was a bludgeon made of wood or stone. Sir Joseph Banks, the famous botanist accompanying Cook, described the weapon as "most admirably calculated for the cracking of sculls (sic)." Concerning the haka, Banks wrote, "Nothing is omittd (sic) which can render a human shape frightful and deformed." The haka, however, was more a bravado-bullying rally than actual attack. When a warrior in a canoe displayed his naked buttocks for the benefit of the English sailors, Cook's surgeon, William Monkhouse, called it "the usual sign of contempt" and decided to "retort the compliment" and mooned the Maori back. The warrior threw a spear at them, and the English fired a small shot, frightening the warriors. As Monkhouse described, "They felt the sting of our laughing at them" and went back to their haka dance.

A few days before the "baring of arses" incident, Cook and his men met with a band of warriors at another bay and were trading peacefully, until one of the warriors made off with an English sword. Cook ordered a small pellet shot fired at him, intended to wound and frighten. Although bleeding, the Maori defiantly waved the sword in the air. Cook then ordered Monkhouse to shoot to kill, which he did.

This mode of operation was typical of the esteemed Captain. Tony Horwitz wrote in *Blue Latitudes*, "Cook would hew to this carefully calibrated escalation during tense moments throughout his Pacific career, with considerable success, until he lost control of himself and his situation early one morning on a beach in Hawaii."

This Hawaiian incident took place ten years later—February 14, 1779—on Cook's third voyage to the Pacific. After unsuccessfully searching for a northwest passage, he and his men had sailed south to reprovision and ended up at Kealakekua Bay on the Big Island. After many weeks there, they left, but were compelled to return three days later for urgent mast repairs. It would prove a fatal decision; they had outstayed their welcome, having eaten the islanders' food and consorted with their women. Cook awoke on the fourth morning of his return to find that the *Resolution*'s largest cutter had been stolen. He ordered his marines to blockade the bay and fire the cannons at canoes. After loading his double-barreled "piece," he went ashore with ten men and marched into the hut of the king of the village. Previously, Cook had been successful with taking a hostage until items were returned, so with the sleepy king in hand, he headed back to the ship. At about the same time, some marines from Cook's second ship, the *Discovery*, went ashore on a launch and shot a chief. On the shoreline, a mob of several thousand gathered, and a skirmish broke out. Cook was beaten and then stabbed to death, along with four other marines. Seventeen Hawaiians, including four chiefs, were killed.

Cook's body was cooked, the flesh removed, and the bones placed in a wicker basket with red feathers, in the custom fit for the highest *ali'i*, or kings. The Hawaiians knew Cook was an important leader and that his bones held particularly great *mana*; they became revered objects. Other parts of Cook's body were returned to the *Resolution* and then buried at sea. Ironically, Cook was not killed in turbulent New Zealand but on the island of Hawai'i, where he had been treated like a blessing from the *akua* (spirit) of the god Lono at the end of Makahiki, the season of fertility.

One of the greatest explorers of all time, not only did Cook put Hawai'i on a chart but his atlases are fairly accurate even by today's standards. Sailing over two hundred thousand miles, Cook redrew the map of the world. But not all revere him. As one Hawaiian asked, "What were we before Cook discovered us, lost?"

Over the next sixty years, contact with Europeans decimated the Hawaiian islanders' population; estimated to have started at 683,000, it went down to just 70,000. Like Native Americans, the isolated Hawaiians had no immunity to European diseases.

At Kealakekua Bay, where Cook died, a white obelisk stands as a memorial. Graffiti on its sides say "Whitey Go Home" and "Captain Crook."

Near a carved-wood building at the cultural center, Paulette and I spoke with one of the performers, Tehinga, originally from New Zealand. Tall and fit, with a shaved head and a penciled-on face tattoo, he was a graduate of the nearby Brigham Young University–Hawaii and was working to pay off college bills. I asked him about the little statue of the man on top of the Maori A-frame building. With expertise in South Pacific studies, he informed us, "The statue is a depiction of Kupe, the father of the Maori people, who embarked from the Taputapuatea[21] temple on the island of Raiatea—called Hawaiki in the middle of the tenth century—near Tahiti, and sailed south until he found Aotearoa, 'Land of the long white cloud,' so

---

21. In 2017, Taputapuatea, a massive stone temple complex, was named a UNESCO World Heritage site.

named because of the clouds or the snow on the mountaintops." Tehinga told us of Kupe's voyage to Hawai'i, which he found had already been settled. He explained that the Polynesian people originated at a place called Hawaiki, or a variation of this name, found throughout the islands. "'Avaiki, Cook Islands, Savai'i Samoa . . . ," Tehinga said.

Standing tall in the bright sunshine outside the Maori hut, wearing a black-and-white beaded skirt, his bare chest emblemed with tattoos, Tehinga broke into an ancient Maori chant:

I haere mai taua i Hawaiki
Tawhiti nui, Tawhiti roa,
Tawhiti Pamamao
I te hono i wai rua

"It means 'You and I have come from Hawaiki, a great distance away, an extended distance away, an extremely remote distance away, even from the joining of the two waters,'" he said, wiping the sweat off his brow. "Perhaps Central America, where the Atlantic and Pacific meet."

Scientists have come to various conclusions on the settling of Polynesia and are still finding new data using archaeological carbon dating. The sweet potato, the staff of life of the Polynesians (called *'uala* in Hawai'i, *kumara* in New Zealand, and *umara* in Tahiti), is, outside of Polynesia, indigenous only to the Americas and parts of Asia. Its possible South American origin was one of the factors that inspired the Norwegian Thor Heyerdahl's Kon-Tiki expedition.[22]

22. *Heyerdahl also based his hypothesis off the fact that on Easter Island, there are reeds, with which the people made their rafts, that are only otherwise found near Lake Titicaca in Peru, and that statues found in the Marquesas bear designs seen only in South America.*

In 1947, he and five other men set sail from Peru in a balsa-wood raft. One hundred and one days later, they landed 4,300 miles away at Raroia in the Tuamotu Islands chain, and Heyerdahl concluded that it was the South Americans who had brought the sweet potato to Polynesia.

I was reminded of a conversation I'd had with Dr. Yosihiko Sinoto, a well-known archaeologist and the senior anthropologist of the Bishop Museum in Honolulu. The polite professor told me that Heyerdahl's theory was almost right, but that it is the other way around: "The Polynesians sailed *to* South America and brought the potato back with them." Sinoto hypothesized a voyage against the wind, in the opposite direction of Heyerdahl's Kon-Tiki expedition. After many digs in Hawai'i and the Marquesas Islands, Sinoto has come to the conclusion that Marquesans settled in Hawai'i in aproximately AD 500.

According to Peter H. Buck, anthropologist and curator of the Bishop Museum in the 1930s, Polynesia was settled by a Stone Age Europoid[23] people who deserve to rank among the world's great navigators, having traveled long distances in their swift catamarans, surpassing the Phoenicians in the Mediterranean and the Vikings in the North Atlantic. Buck, whose mother was Maori, writes in his book *Vikings of the Sunrise*, "Yet long before Columbus made his great voyage, a stone-age people, in efficient crafts, had crossed the Pacific from continent to continent across its widest part and had colonized every habitable island within its vast interior."

---

23. *Also called Caucasian. Of the three basic groups of people—Mongoloid, Negroid, and Europoid—the Polynesians fall into the last group by their physical characteristics. Buck wrote, "They have not the woolly hair and broad nose of the Negroid nor the flat face and drooping inner eyefold of the Mongoloid."*

Even before the Vikings' Leif Erikson, son of Erik the Red, discovered the eastern coast of North America, the Polynesians, those intrepid mariners, had sailed the vast Pacific Ocean, navigating by the stars. Over hundreds and even thousands of years, the islanders mixed. They came from Tahiti and the Marquesas, and sailed up to Hawai'i, down to New Zealand, and back up. Why not over to America, or vice versa?

Because of phonetic similarities in the Polynesian and Indonesian languages, many scientists believe that the Polynesians originally migrated from somewhere in Southeast Asia. The bottom line is that Polynesia (whose name comes from the Greek words *poly*, "many," and *nesos*, "islands") was settled by several migrating peoples from Asia and America who mixed over thousands of years.

At an open-air hut in the Maori village at the center, we watched a man with a mallet and chisel shape wood planks into intricate carved sidings that would soon adorn the houses of the faux village. After admiring the sculpture collection, I saw a koa spear and picked it up. Green-blue eyes stared back at me from the head with pencil-thin designs carved into it.

"It's from this," said the carver, holding out a piece of thin shell. Although he was of Maori heritage, the man's eyes matched the shell's color. He introduced himself as Doug and showed me other fine sculptures, some old, from former village carvers, including his father.

When he returned to the workshop to wrap the spear for me, a woman who introduced herself as Auntie Vea wrote up the bill. She said that she had worked at the center since the sixties and that she had known Elvis and even shaken hands with him. "He sweat so much, his shirt was always drenched wet. You remember his famous Blaisdell Arena concert in 1973?" she said.

"Aloha from Hawaii broadcasted around the world," I replied.

"Elvis donated most of the money from that concert to build the *Arizona* Memorial. And he had that home in Pūpūkea practically carved into the hill. Ah, Elvis! He was one of us," Auntie Vea said.

After watching the grand flotilla of canoes full of singers and dancers, Paulette and I left the village. I didn't see anyone who remotely resembled Elvis.

CHAPTER TWENTY-TWO

'Iolani Palace

*I have always said that under our own system in former
days there was always plenty for prince or for people.*
—QUEEN LILI'UOKALANI, *HAWAI'I'S STORY*, 1898

Hawai'i is home to three royal palaces: Queen Emma's Summer Palace
in Nu'uanu on O'ahu; the Hulihe'e Palace in Kailua-Kona on the Big
Island; and the biggest one in the United States, the 'Iolani Palace
in Honolulu. Still on holiday there, we drove along the waterfront
near the Ala Moana shopping center, skirted the harbor, and passed
the Aloha Tower Marketplace. We turned inland a few blocks before
Chinatown, parked, and walked through the iron gates of 'Iolani.

Our docent, an elderly gentleman named Donald Ching, gave
us cloth slippers to pull over our shoes, explaining to our group of
twenty—some of them tourists, some locals—that the curators didn't
want the beautifully polished wooden floors to be scratched. He
said, "The palace has been restored to its original splendor. Built at
a cost of $360,000 in 1882, the 'Iolani Palace had electricity before

the White House. On his voyage back to Hawai'i from Europe, King Kalakaua had a fortuitous meeting in New York with Thomas Edison, and the king was soon flipping switches to electric chandeliers in his island palace."

As we walked through its halls, we admired the portraits of European kings and queens, gifts to the monarchy of the "Sandwich Islands."[24] Paulette, being of French nationality, gravitated toward a painting of Louis-Philippe I and then studied a silver sword, a gift from Napoleon III, hanging on the wall.

After visiting the palaces of Europe, King Kalakaua built his own, grand enough to elicit respect among visiting dignitaries, so as not to be dismissed as a "savage." His palace boasts columns, moldings, leaded-glass windows imported from San Francisco, and an abundance of Victorian decor. Originally called Hale Ali'i (House of the Chiefs), it was changed during Kamehameha V's reign to 'Iolani, which literally means "Royal Hawk," a native bird from Kohala, the Big Island, near our house.

Kalakaua had seen the gold crowns worn by royals in Europe, so upon returning to Hawai'i, he concluded that his old feather helmet lacked sufficient majesty. He arranged for a coronation ceremony in which, since he was already king, he crowned himself with gold.

At the time, the islands' sugar industry was flourishing. American businessmen, Sanford B. Dole in particular, wanted Hawai'i to become a US territory, to lift heavy import taxes levied on sugar. Dole had allies among Hawaiian businessmen who believed Lili'uokalani, next in line for the throne, would be incapable of running the government. Two years after the death of Kalakaua in 1891, the US Navy

---

24. *Captain Cook named Hawai'i after his longtime Admiralty patron the Earl of Sandwich, who was immortalized by his request for a piece of meat between two pieces of bread—an invention from then on known as a sandwich.*

staged a coup. The queen quickly ceded the throne, not wanting her people killed, believing that the president of the United States would restore the monarchy upon learning of this outrage. Loyal Hawaiians resisted, and the navy took her prisoner. "She was charged with treason in her own empire," Mr. Ching said, as he led us into the spartan bedroom where Queen Lili'uokalani was held during her house arrest.

There was a military cot, a simple desk, and a cabinet where she kept a meager supply of food. Mr. Ching then broke into a heartfelt song in Hawaiian, whose words had been written by the musically gifted queen in that very room. In the song, she forgives her tormentors for the sin of imprisoning her. In 1898, the United States, preoccupied with the Spanish–American War, annexed Hawai'i as a strategic naval base for the Pacific theater.

After the tour, my wife spoke with Donald Ching. They are both of Chinese descent, and she asked him what kind he was, "Hakka or Punti?" He chuckled and said, "Only another islander would make this distinction. Those Chinese whose ancestors migrated to Hawai'i and Tahiti and other remote parts of the world more than one hundred years ago are living in somewhat of a time warp."

The two groups were old rivals from the provinces of the Yellow River basin in northern China—known as China proper in ancient times, as opposed to Manchuria and Mongolia. The sturdy Hakka were from the foothills; the more sophisticated Punti from the lowlands. Their rivalry recalls the historical tensions between Florentines and Sienese, or the Crow and Blackfoot.

A week after our visit, a letter arrived from Donald; enclosed was a fascinating article about the migrations of the Hakka Chinese all over the world, explaining that the Chinese originally came to Hawai'i to work in the sugarcane and pineapple fields, but after a few years began to excel in trade. The many shops still prospering in Honolulu's Chinatown are evidence of their mercantile skill.

That night back in Honolulu, while we waited for a table at Duke's, we admired old photos of surfers, canoe paddlers, and of course Duke Kahanamoku posing with everybody who was anybody in Waikīkī. On the beach under the moonlight, we savored sashimi and were serenaded by singers strumming ukuleles. "Do you think Honolulu is an interesting city?" Paulette asked.

"Well, it has its own social hierarchy, a mixture of descendants of *ali'i*, missionaries, Portuguese, prosperous Asians, upwardly mobile Filipinos, and Samoans." After all the museums and touring, I was overflowing with island info.

"Where else can one visit a royal palace, surf, and go horseback riding on a ranch all in one day?" she asked.

"Sri Lanka?" I guessed.

"And order kava in a bar, hear a symphony, and dine on the beach while viewing the lights of a big city?

"In the middle of winter—only in Hawai'i!" we chanted.

CHAPTER TWENTY-THREE

Pearl Harbor and American Samurais

We have awakened a sleeping giant and have instilled in him a terrible resolve.

—Admiral Isoroku Yamamoto, after the attack on Pearl Harbor

Most Hawaiians of a certain age personally remember December 7, 1941, "a date which will live in infamy," as Franklin D. Roosevelt said the day after the bombing of Pearl Harbor. Back on the Big Island, I was sitting on a bench in the cool, clean town of Waimea reading the paper while Paulette shopped nearby. An elderly Hawaiian woman motored up, parked her scooter chair next to me, and started a lively conversation. Her name was Abigail, from Oʻahu. Did she remember Pearl Harbor?

"Oh, yah, I was in high school, out on a field playing before class started and shouted, 'Look! There are planes coming down from

the sky!' And one of my friends said, 'Are you drunk or something?' And then there was shooting and chaos everywhere. We were scared for months afterward, especially with the blackouts. We carried gas masks along with our books to school."

Another old woman, who was in charge at the transfer station where I unloaded garbage, told me she was working at the cafeteria on Hickam Air Force Base on that fateful day. She said, "I remember seeing people, even civilians, shot down . . . my friends . . ." The poor woman started to cry, the memories too painful.

My insurance broker, Tad Nottage, told me that his father saw a group of Japanese fighter planes bombing the naval air station on the east side of O'ahu. "He had gotten up early to go exploring on a high bluff above Kane'ohe and saw three planes coming in, right over the house. He said they were so low he could see the goggles on the faces of the pilots and big red circles on the wings. He thought it was some kind of exercise until my grandmother pulled him back inside and said, 'It's on the radio. It's war.'"

"So how old was your father at the time?" I asked.

"Only thirteen. And he told me, 'There was smoke everywhere. All the seaplanes were on fire, and the hangars too,'" Tad said. "You really ought to see the *Arizona* Memorial. It's quite an experience."

In 1941, after years of disagreement with Japan during its empire expansion that began with its conquest of Manchuria in 1931, Roosevelt declared an embargo on all exports to the country. Diplomatic peace talks reached a standoff, but meetings were to resume in Washington with the Japanese ambassador on December 7, 1941. The sudden attack on Pearl Harbor on that very day catapulted the United States into war with the Empire of Japan. "The sleeping giant" that was America, made up of both military personnel and civilians, became unified in a way never seen before. Together, all Americans worked toward victory with vigor and a motivating motto, Remember Pearl Harbor.

On our next trip to the big city, we caught a cab and walked into the entrance of the Pearl Harbor Visitor Center. We purchased our tickets for the USS *Arizona* Memorial tour from a man in uniform, passed the giant anchor and chain of the USS *Arizona*, and were ushered into a small theater. A female park ranger lectured, "The *Arizona* is a monument for those 2,390 men who lost their lives when the Japanese wiped out almost our entire Pacific navy fleet, including nineteen warships and six airfields. Our liberty today is owed to all Americans of the 'Greatest Generation.' This memorial is not just for those who died here but also for the tens of thousands who lost their lives in bloody battles all over the Pacific, from the backwaters

of Bougainville to Guadalcanal. You are now on hallowed ground. Please keep your voices at a whisper; it is a cemetery. One thousand one hundred and seventy-seven men are still buried in the ship down at the bottom of the sea. Some of us even have family here; my own mother's fiancé was a musician practicing with the navy band when the bombs landed on that Sunday morning at 7:00 a.m. Pearl Harbor was the beginning of the war in the Pacific, and is also a symbol of its end, with the USS *Missouri* docked in perpetuity next to the *Arizona*. And now," she added, "let's watch the movie."

The lights dimmed, and an old documentary flickered. The black-and-white footage showed the Japanese bombers flying in from their carriers two hundred miles off O'ahu for the surprise attack. The Japanese had launched 350 planes—high-level bombers, torpedo bombers, and dive bombers—in disciplined swarms. As their bombs fell on the *Arizona*'s ammunition storage, the ship exploded in a cloud of black smoke. It was a powerful film, but to watch it at Pearl Harbor itself was overwhelming. Many in the audience wept openly, and others trembled in their seats. After the half-hour movie ended, there was reverential silence.

We exited the theater and boarded a forty-five-foot navy launch, which ferried us across the lagoon the Hawaiians once called Wai Momi, meaning "Water of Pearls," after the pearl oysters that thrived there. The navy captain docked the launch in front of the long white building on pilings built over the wreck of the *Arizona*, and we climbed a ramp to the openly designed memorial. From every angle, we could see the rusted bones of the six-hundred-foot-long ship, sunken in the silt on the lagoon's shallow bottom. Rainbow-colored bubbles rose to the sea's surface—oil *still* seeps from the *Arizona*'s tanks. On the back wall at the far end of a well-lit room, I read the names of dead soldiers. Three Conrads were on the list. Distant relatives perhaps?

There was a commotion in the back of the group, and some of us were horrified to see people who looked Japanese laughing loudly and snapping pictures of one another. When the guard told them to be quiet or they would be escorted out, they didn't understand either the English or the Japanese translation. They were from another Asian country, but they got the idea and shut up.

After seeing the *Arizona*, we took a bus over a small bridge to Ford Island to tour the USS *Missouri*. The *Missouri* was the last battleship to be commissioned by the navy during World War II. It actually remained seaworthy long enough to fire shots in 1991 in the Persian Gulf War.

Rather than risking hundreds of thousands more Allied troops fighting on Japan's home turf, President Truman chose to drop atomic bombs on Hiroshima and Nagasaki. The Japanese conceded defeat on August 14, 1945, and the formal surrender terms were signed on September 2 aboard the *Missouri* in Tokyo Bay.

Paulette and I were abuzz on war memorabilia, so the next morning, we walked through Waikīkī to Fort DeRussy and into the US Army Museum of Hawaii. There we shook hands with the white-bearded historian Pierre Moulin, originally from the town of Bruyères in the Vosges Mountains, France, which was almost completely destroyed by the Nazis. Monsieur Moulin said, "My grandfather helped build the monument honoring all those who died, and I brought the model of it here to Hawai'i to share the history of my village and the 442nd Regimental Combat Team, made up of Japanese from Hawai'i and from the detention camps on the West Coast. In June 1944, they joined the 100th Infantry in the most important battle in the history of war."

"How so?" I asked.

"Two hundred and eleven soldiers of the 36th Texan Division were surrounded, and the 'American samurais'—you know, some of these soldiers were actual descendants of samurais, and their motto was Go for Broke—not only pushed through the German lines but also held their ground in a different kind of fight; this was close to the border. The Germans used every trick in the book—and they *wrote* the book: booby traps, mines, screaming meemies, tree-burst artillery fire, *toutes les choses*," Pierre said, reverting to French as he had been chatting with Paulette. (She told him that she'd met Charles de Gaulle when he came to Tahiti in 1966.)

"One of the Texans later said, 'The Germans hit us from one flank, then the other, then the front and the rear. We were never so glad to see anyone as those fighting Japanese Americans.' When President Harry Truman welcomed the surviving soldiers of the 442nd, he said, 'You fought for the free nations of the world. . . . You fought not only the enemy, but you fought prejudice—and you have won.'"

While waiting to get my signed copy of *American Samurais WWII in Europe*, I read "In September 1943, the 100th Infantry Battalion, made up primarily of the Hawaiian National Guard, landed in Salerno, Italy. They proved themselves among other units, liberating the roads to Rome held by the Germans. Within six months, 600 of the 1,400 soldiers had died."

I asked Pierre about Daniel Inouye, who served forty-nine years in the Senate and had lost his right arm and been awarded the Bronze Star Medal.

Pierre said, "Along with fifty-two others of the 442nd, he earned the Distinguished Service Cross, and also the Medal of Honor. And this is an unusual thing to say about a politician: he was honest. And he was my best friend." Pierre's voice cracked on that last sentence, and when he leaned back, I realized I hadn't until that moment noticed, because of the stacks of his books, that he was in a wheelchair.

Once back at our Big Island home, we watched World War II movies and discussed the historical impact of the war. Paulette, a French citizen, had a new perspective on her adopted country. I even serenaded her with our national anthem, accompanied by my twanging guitar, after playing "Tiny Bubbles."

"The Big Pineapple is an amazing American city. With its World War II sites, drive-ins with old neon lights, and Asian restaurants, it's Disneyland, New York City, Saigon, Papeete, and Tokyo all combined," I said.

"Like certain foods mixed with poi in a calabash," Paulette replied, while frying up some *chao fan*.

"Heh, how about wild-hog burgers topped with slices of pine-apple?" I said.

CHAPTER TWENTY-FOUR

Spam, Poke, and Kava

That's the thing about food from Hawai'i. It lights up people's hearts and eyes.

—SAM CHOY, *THE CHOY OF COOKING*, 1996

Spam, a contraction of "spiced ham," the lunch-meat product that fell out of favor in the 1950s in most of America, is still going strong in the Aloha State. The canned meat from Austin, Minnesota, was introduced to Hawai'i by the military and was appreciated because it kept well in the tropics. Today, Hawai'i consumes over four million cans of Spam per year, more than any other state. Hormel Foods markets a Spam Hawaii Collector's Edition, its label sporting two hula dolls and slices of fried Spam wrapped with seaweed. In Hawai'i, some people eat Spam and eggs for breakfast, Spam and rice for lunch, and grilled pineapple with Spam for dinner.

Surprisingly, the mixture of Spam and certain foods makes for a delicious combination. At my son's soccer games, *musubi* (a block of rice topped with sliced grilled Spam and wrapped in seaweed) was the favorite snack. As a soccer dad commissioned to provide refreshments for the team, I found myself ordering thirty portions at a local deli. (Remember the Monty Python skit where the waitress says, "Egg and Spam; egg, bacon, and Spam," and the choir of comedians sings, "Spam! Spam! Spam! Spam! Lovely Spam! Lovely Spam!" and a restaurant customer unsuccessfully tries to order something not containing Spam?)

Hawai'i's mucilaginous poi, a gray paste made of cooked taro roots, is generally considered uninteresting (some would say) on its own, but with Spam, it is transformed into a savory dish.

As for poke (pronounced "poh-kay"), it is Hawaiian soul food, and the best place to dip one's chopsticks into it is at the Hawaii Poke Festival.

Paulette and I bought tickets to Sam Choy's Poke Contest and walked into the conference room of one of the nearby hotels that dot the Kona Coast. Food-laden tables, adorned with flowers, had dishes elaborately displayed—with water fountains, painted backdrops, glass sculptures, models of volcanoes and fishing villages, even miniature oriental gardens with tiny bridges. We ran into Kavika, one of our neighbors. He was one of the sixty-two judges who had the enviable two-hour-long job of sampling the tasty dishes, sometimes twice, before casting their vote. His wife, Kathy, pointed to his belly and said, "He's well equipped for the job."

The annual competition features traditional poke dishes as well as some of the wildest combinations imaginable. Categories include Professional, Amateur, Traditional, and Improvisational.

Poke consists of bite-sized pieces of fish, most commonly ahi tuna or marlin, marinated in a sauce—traditionally containing salt, seaweed, soy sauce, and sesame oil. It can be served up as lunch, a snack, or an appetizer. One chef made Mexican-style poke, with refried beans and hot salsa. It was a tasty twist on ceviche, and—*olé!*—it was *magnifico*. One woman from Iowa used corn to reflect her heritage, while an Alaskan used salmon. A daring amateur even submitted a poke dish featuring both Spam and poi.

Sam Choy, wearing a triple-extra-large flower-patterned aloha shirt, circulated among the tables with the other judges. He is one top chef who is unashamed to use Spam, and plans on publishing a Spam cookbook one day. He narrowed the field down to five, excluding the dish with Spam. His favorite in the Amateur division used only local premissionary ingredients. "This is one real Kona-style poke dish—pre-Captain Cook," he said.

Some traditional recipes rely on hard-to-gather ingredients, such as certain reef fish, octopus ink, various types of *limu* (seaweed), and raw limpets known as *opihi*, a favorite of turtles as well as poke gourmets. All of the dishes at the contest were so delicious that we ourselves were transformed into poke gourmands; we began eating it at least twice a week.

If we don't buy one of the many store-made varieties, we prepare poke at home. Our basic recipe is straightforward:

POKE

8 ounces fresh ahi tuna
1 tbsp chopped fresh ogo (edible seaweed)
1 tbsp green onion, chopped
1 tbsp sweet Maui onion (or white onion) chopped

2 tbsp soy sauce

1 tsp toasted sesame oil

Cut tuna into bite-sized one-inch cubes. Combine the remaining ingredients in a small bowl and mix well. Pour the sauce over the tuna and combine well. Chill until serving. Serves four.

Here's how we do it Tahitian-style:

POISSON CRU

---

1 pound fresh ahi tuna (preferably block)

1/4 Maui sweet onion, sliced very thin

1/2 green bell pepper, sliced into fine matchsticks

1 carrot, finely shredded

1/2 cucumber, peeled and thinly sliced

1/2 cup fresh lime juice (about 4 limes)

4 tbsp sugar

1 1/2 tsp salt

1/2 cup coconut milk (optional)

Cut the fish into strips three inches by 1/2-inch. Arrange the fish and the vegetables on a platter. In a bowl, combine the lime juice, sugar, and salt. Pour this dressing on the tuna-vegetable combination and mix well. Let it rest 5 minutes, then add coconut milk and serve immediately. Serves four.

This raw fish dish is versatile. You may wish to add chopped tomatoes, chopped green onions, pickled daikon, pickled ginger, et cetera. *Poisson cru* made with fresh mahi-mahi is delicious as the lime juice, in effect, cooks the fish. (Think ceviche.)

We were now inspired to try everything Hawaiian. While Paulette shopped for local ingredients at the farmers' market, I did some "stepping out" to drink—not booze but the ancient Hawaiian beverage *'awa*, known mostly throughout the Pacific as kava.

Thirty minutes north of our house, in the small town of Hawi, I walked to the back of a century-old building and into the Kava Café. The bartender was stirring a large wooden bowl on the counter, ladling muddy-looking water into coconut half shells for customers at the bar. Others who already had their bowls were lounging on the old couch and easy chairs. I recognized one of them: Hap, a wood craftsman from whom I'd bought a koa bookshelf. Still covered in sawdust, he was sipping from a coconut bowl. We shook hands, I took a seat on a stool, and Keoni, the *'awa* bartender, handed me a bowl. Its contents tasted pasty, with a hint of an earthy root suggesting ginger and a peppery tang. "It's not for the taste, but the effect," Keoni explained. "This isn't that potent, but it should relax you a bit."

It did. My shoulders immediately felt looser, and I slouched in the chair and listened to the amiable island chatter. My mouth went numb and dropped open. A certain contented indolence overtook me. After the soothing physical effect came a feeling of camaraderie, even for the old man slouched in the corner; never mind his terrible teeth—he was now my brother!

The conversation took on a lighter tone. Jokes were mumbled, including ones about aging. The fellow with the bad teeth said, "One thing I know is that I'm not as fast now as I was." Not funny, but we all laughed. The ice was broken and the kava brotherhood ensued. Some of us were more listeners, others chatterers. Tom, an engineer, talked about canoe paddling and said that the slouching old man was his father from Oʻahu, a retired navy man. The old man then pulled out of his jacket pocket a newspaper clipping of his son paddling in the Molokaʻi race from some years back.

Another Hawaiian man came in, shook hands with everyone, chugged a cup, said, "Aloha," and walked out.

Hap said, "He drinks kava every day to clear his head. Says it's better than booze, which clouds it up."

A bunch of dried kava roots, looking like wooden sticks, were pinned to the wall. Keoni explained that the roots, from the pepper shrub *Piper methysticum*, are ground into a powder and then strained. "A woman's nylon stocking works best," he said and fished out what looked like a salami from the brown kava water—a stocking tied at either end, full of the brown kava powder.

"Fill the stocking with about an ounce—half a sandwich baggie full—of the kava powder, and put it into a gallon of water in a bowl. Knead it until the water turns a silty brown color, then you're ready for about sixteen single cups."

Time had lapsed seamlessly. Before saying goodbye, I begged to buy a bag of kava powder if Keoni could spare some.

Once home, however, I couldn't find anyone to get stoned with me, and I didn't feel like getting buzzed alone. My wife said sensibly, "You're nuts."

One afternoon, I rummaged through her drawers for a nylon stocking. I put the earthy powder in it, tied the ends, and kneaded the silty elixir in a bowl of water. After much pestering and convincing her of the health benefits, she finally joined me for a cup on the back porch. The evening sun hit the tops of the snowcapped Mauna Kea as we sipped our concoction. It was clearly different than sipping Pinot Noir or Cabernet and comparing bouquets or flavors with hints of robust cherry or oak overtones. At least it tasted better than the pungent noni juice.

We fell into a contented mellowness. I poured a glass of red wine to have with dinner. "What are you drinking?" Paulette asked.

I meant to say Cabernet, but with a numbed mouth it came out "kavanet."

Perhaps kava, a mild narcotic, is a naturally occurring tropical Prozac. It has been the mainstay of South Pacific medicine for over a thousand years, used variously as an appetite suppressant and a decongestant, as well as to control blood pressure, relieve stress, and promote longevity. It is also taken for certain customs and rituals, but not every day. It is said in the islands that if you become a big kava-head and drink vast quantities of the stuff, you will hear voices in the wind and perhaps even a long-departed ancestor telling you to dance the hula like a crazed wild turkey.

Staring up at the stars, I fancied that I had connected with the earth in a spiritual way. I had wonderful thoughts but couldn't find the words for them. That night, I slept like a log.

CHAPTER TWENTY-FIVE

Our Island Home

*People elsewhere said how distant I was, and off the map,
but no—they were far away, still groping onward. I was at
last where I wanted to be. I had proved what I had always
suspected, that even the crookedest journey is the way home.*
—PAUL THEROUX, *HOTEL HONOLULU*, 2001

We were finally ready to have a luau.

People arrived from all over the island. We'd invited friends from surfing, fishing, and canoe paddling; children who attended Will's school, along with their parents; and all of the people who had worked on the house and garden. We dug a hole in the ground and made a fire with kiawe wood to heat stones for the *imu*, a traditional underground oven. The food was wrapped in banana leaves, and there were generous portions of poke, sashimi, *limu*, taro, and yams, as well as local spinach with coconut sauce. There was *opihi*, the limpets from the ocean, along with ono, ahi, and *tako*. Lalamilo supplied a fresh wild pig.

The first guests were sipping their wine on the back porch when I spotted Jedi dragging the roasting pig out of the *imu* by its hind leg, Will chasing after her. She was halfway across the lawn before he could stop her from ruining the main course. She ripped off one of the pig's legs. Will reached for her collar, but she grabbed the piece of meat in her jaws and disappeared into the jungle. I walked over, and just as I was making a Maori "ugly face," my fishing buddy Mario said, "No problem, brah." He poured beer over the three-legged pig, washing off the dirt, and carried it back to the oven. Lalamilo ambled over with one of his Filipino workers who had come along to help out with the *imu*.

"You like I wok da dog?" Lalamilo said, winking.

"Make Pilipino hot dog?" said the worker.

"I can always get another kine pig from back dere," Lalamilo said, pointing to the jungle, "'cept have to wait until early morning." He moved his fist and arm up and down, pantomiming, as if holding a machete.

A couple who had recently purchased a fancy beachfront house nearby left after the pig incident. "Dey snobs," growled Mario. They missed out on a delicious meal, especially the earthy smoked pork that was so tender it just fell off the bone.

There were other snafus, such as when someone carrying a bowl of poi tripped on the cord to the electric bass of the island-style band we had hired and the pasty glob stuck to a woman's hair. Nevertheless, we all drank and hulaed happily and had a fine time at the luau.

After we opened up our house to the islanders, I noticed that neighbors no longer referred to our homestead as "the old architect's house" but as "the Conrads' place." We had become *kamaʻāina*, belonging to the land.

Many people dream of living on an island, yet several mainlanders asked us, as if we lived on Mars, "What is there to do out there?" Sometimes it does feel as if we're on another planet, as the vast surrounding ocean isolates us from other continents. We tell them about "Maui watching"; many living on our side of the Big Island make it a ritual to gather on the beach to watch the sunset burnish the distant silhouette of Maui to the northwest. The sun leaves the sky looking as if it were rubbed with gold dust. A green flash sometimes rises above the spot where the sun sinks below the horizon: light refracted off the moisture above the seawater. Some people think it simple-minded to ponder a sunset; for me, it is an appropriate time to reflect on the joys of life.

When one lives on an island, there is something comforting in seeing other islands in the distance, to know we are not alone. Even whales tire of the empty ocean, seeking out Maui and then the island of Hawai'i before migrating back to the Pacific Northwest coast and up to Alaska.

On a clear day, from just the right angle, we can see the forty-five-square-mile island of Kaho'olawe. A hundred years ago, goats and cattle ate its vegetation, and the island became barren. Then, beginning in World War II, this circle in the sea was used by the military for target practice and bomb tests. Groups of Hawaiians protested and sued the government, and in 1990, the navy halted nearly fifty years of bomb testing and returned Kaho'olawe to the native Hawaiians. Now the small island is a cultural preserve, and reforestation is slowly healing its topography.[25]

---

25. *It cost over four hundred million dollars to clean up the island. In the process, archaeologists uncovered a treasury of relics: some three thousand ancient settlements, artifacts, and petroglyphs.*

Many *malahini* (newcomers) complain that there are no seasons in Hawai'i. Not true; it's just that the seasonal changes are subtle. In the winter, a cool breeze blows from the snowcapped mountains, and there is the loud sound of humpback whales breaching just off the reef. In the summer, a moist, warm wind comes in from the south, and the smell of ginger and gardenias blooming permeates the air. And it is mango season; islanders get more excited about that fruit of paradise than the English do over a cup of Earl Grey. Sometimes Will accompanied me on mango quests, catching them with a burlap sack to keep them from bruising on the ground after I climbed up the trees on nearby properties and tossed mangoes down to him. With bags dangling from our bicycles and with backpacks full, we trudged home with our loot—to be chilled for desserts or whipped into mango smoothies. We gave them away to neighbors up and down the block, who received the delicacy with many mahalos.

As for time of day, we tell that differently on the islands, too. My wife has always been an early riser—up at the hour when finches fart—while I usually awake around the time doves coo. Then I hear the clicking snicker of the geckos as they climb the walls. I doze until I hear the herons by the pond screeching, "Aarch-aarch-aarch!" Then there is the francolin's[26] shrill yodel, "Yiddle-yiddle-yiddle!" A flock of wild turkeys scream, "Yobble, yobble, yobble!" Along with the babbling pandemonium of the myna birds that nest in the eaves of our roof and the cardinals singing from the trees, they form a choir louder than the Mormon Tabernacle's. That's how I know it's about seven thirty.

Depending on the tide and the swell, the surf makes distinct sounds. During the winter months, on the days when the swell is up,

---

26. *The francolin partridge from North Africa was brought to Hawai'i as a game bird.*

the waves pounding the shore seem to say, "I'm big and powerful, but bursting with fun," as they explode on the reef. They swoosh up on the sand and retreat quickly, as if to taunt, "Catch me if you can!" In the summer, on our northwest side of the island, the surf subsides and laps the shore with a sound like "Hush, hush." This is the season to snorkel, fish, and paddle canoes and kayaks.

In the evenings, after dining alfresco on our back lanai, I watch the myriad stars on the black-velvet dome above. With no city light causing urban nightglow, stargazing in Hawai'i's clear, dark nights is astonishing. Sometimes *pueo*, white island owls, flutter across the sparkly view; settling in the trees and swiveling their round feathered faces, they coo. The soporific fragrance from our tropical garden is like a perfume. The breeze on my skin feels like a caress as soft as a woman's fine hair, and the waves breaking on the coral seem to whisper, "Nothing more to do, nothing more to do."

Sometimes, when I'd think of the city life I'd left, it seemed I was only dreaming that I was there in the islands. The months had slipped by and turned into years. Mainland friends and places where I had worked receded into the remote shadows of memory.

Home is what the island had become to me. The beauty of the beach made the days more soulful, and the ebb and flow of the tidal pools comforted me. Most people who make a long journey can't wait to get back home and tell everyone about it. But this sabbatical had turned into a permanent relocation. I was like the man who one day at the office mutters something about a dentist appointment and steps out, never to return. I had essentially vanished from the life I once knew. Was there any reason to go back?

One day, while working in the garden, I mentioned to Lalamilo that perhaps someday I would go back to the mainland to live. He furrowed his eyebrows and shook his head.

"*Hele* from Havai'i? What fo'? You *kama'āina*, long time here. We all *keiki* o' Havai'i." He pulled a rake across a pile of leaves. "No good over dere, da *'āina haole*."

It sounded like the beginning of another of his meandering philosophical conversations—talking story was one of the bountiful pleasures of life in the islands. He pointed up to the trees full of ripe coconuts and said, "Have plenny coconut over dere?"

"No," I said and shook my head.

"*Mikana?*" he said as he pointed to the row of papaya trees lining the side of the yard. "And *manako*?" He nodded at the little mangoes that were beginning to sprout on the tree we had planted when we first arrived. "And *'ulu*?" He pointed at the breadfruit tree beginning to fan out its elephantine leaves. "And *maiʻa*?" The green and yellow bananas growing off the dark-purple stems on the sturdy green stalks. "And poi and fish like ono and ahi, so fresh like it swim right out of da ocean? And *ha*. The people dere got no *ha*. The breath of life, *ha* as in *aloha*!"

I told Lalamilo that he was right about these things, but what did he know about the mainland life?

"Long time befo', I wen' live on island spit'n distance to mainland," Lalamilo said.

I was surprised, as I had never heard him talk of the mainland, and said, "Catalina? Vancouver Island?"

"No, Man-hat-tan Island," he said, with a sly smile on his lips. "But no tell my *wahine*."

Lalamilo then told me he once married a *haole*, with hair "the color of coconut husks." Off they went to New York, the theater district, where he played the ukulele and sang island songs while his wife danced the hula, which she had learned in Hawaiʻi.

"She dance hula no worth beans, but she had da kine *maoli* tattoos," Lalamilo said. "And *ono* kine papayas . . ." He cupped his hands under his chest.

"After I meet da kine's family, she *hilahila*, shame, say I need lessons, speak English. I say what you t'ink? Only speak Hawaiian? She wen' *huhu*. Whole t'ing *pau*. Den *hoi mai*, I come back." He shrugged his shoulders.

"She one *wahine waha nui*, big mouth. No *akamai*, no smart. Always blah, blah, blah, all same myna bird, but with dat New Yawk accent." He stuck his pinkie finger in his ear and twirled it.

After his stint in New York, he said he never left the islands again. "But now I old. Soon I make da kine voyage—Hawaiki." He said he'd been building a great sailing canoe, on weekends, for the past ten years. "Some day, all *pau*," Lalamilo said. "Den I sail it through the Kealaikahiki channel, da road to Tahiti. *Hele* on to Hawaiki, da place my granfadder tol' me 'bout."

Lalamilo said that his grandfather's grandfather and so on, going back more than forty generations, had passed on the oral tradition of their lost homeland to the southeast, Hawaiki, which lay a three-week sail south.

Lalamilo had earlier announced that he was going to sail away on a full moon, when the wind blew not too cold and not too warm down from Mauna Kea, in the direction of Hōkūle'a, the Star of Gladness.

"Why now?" I asked.

"Cancer. Doc say one mo' year to live," he said. But Lalamilo was never much concerned with time, and almost a year had passed since the diagnosis.

"One way or da odda, I sail Hawaiki Nui," Lalamilo said. He shook my hand and *honi*, hugged me, and slightly brushed his nose against mine in the traditional style of farewell, similar to the *hongi* of New Zealand. He said, "*Aloha nui loa*. You can leave Hawai'i, but Hawai'i will never leave you. Da spirit of Hawai'i, always aloha."

That was the last I saw of Lalamilo. He died a few months later while lying peacefully in his canoe. I will always remember him as a great custodian of the *'āina*, the land, and a master of the *moana*, the sea. I think of him, humorous and kind, puttering around a tropical garden or sailing his canoe in the lagoon, perhaps in the heaven known as Hawaiki.

What is the future of this fragile paradise, our beautiful state of Hawai'i? Does its fate depend simply on "good" development versus "bad"? Currently, too many golf courses prevent the runoff of the natural rivers, and grass-saving insecticides pollute the water around the reefs. And how much population growth can the islands handle before the aloha spirit unravels?

Modernity has its price: O'ahu is overbuilt, and Maui has more hotel rooms than it can fill. Lanai no longer produces pineapples. Ni'ihau is dusty and barren, as cattle have eaten much of the vegetation. The west side of the Big Island—the resort mecca, the playground of the Pacific—is being developed at an incredible pace. Its roads were planned badly, and the two-lane highway belting the island is famous for head-on collisions. It's heartbreaking to see the wilting leis, boogie boards, fishing rods, crosses, and Hawaiian flags along the side of the road, left by teenagers as memorials for friends who have died in fatal crashes there.

These unique islands have been under attack, in one way or another, ever since man set foot on them. The early Hawaiians collected colorful feathers and slaughtered birds, causing many species to go extinct. The state bird, the nene, a type of flightless goose, almost disappeared like the dodo; though still endangered, it now numbers 2,500. With 90 percent of Hawai'i's species found nowhere else, this is their last stand. The islands have lost more indigenous species of plants and birds than any distinct ecosystem on the planet.

One day, I was driving down to Kona on our biweekly shopping trip and turned on the radio. "And now, here's Braddah Iz,"[27] said the familiar voice of the deejay, Kahikina. "Listen, folks, whatever you do dis weekend, don't go to Volcanoes National Forest, cause it's closed—temporarily, yah. Da kine second vent blew. Now der are two *pukas* in da volcano making plenny *pilau* smoke. Visitors

---

27. *The three-hundred-pound Israel Ka'ano'i Kamakawiwo'ole, who died in 1997, was a musical hero in Hawai'i, and remains so.*

have been evacuated, so stay home, yah." (Kilauea has been erupting since 1983, but this second vent releases more sulfur dioxide, a pollutant that is also emitted from burning coal and oil. Local doctors, however, are not certain if the smoky air is any more unhealthful than that of big cities.)

A few months later, the volcano's fuming abated, so we drove south to Hawai'i Volcanoes National Park to see the hot lava. In the evening's golden hour, we followed the winding Chain of Craters Road down to the coast and parked alongside hundreds of other cars on a black gravel area. Once the sun had set, we could see the fiery glow of thick red streams trickling down the mountain. Even though lava brings death to plants and old terrain, it is the birth of land and is incredible to witness. Over the last thirty-five years, the lava flows have spilled into the sea to create an additional 875 acres, the newest land on earth and growing every day. Thirty miles offshore there is an island, which has already been named Lo'ihi, being formed by underwater volcanic eruptions. It will rise to the surface in about ten thousand years.

After seeing the lava lights, we drove to our hotel in the village of Volcano for a late supper and a night's rest. The next morning, we visited the Kilauea Caldera, three miles long and two miles wide. We stood at the edge of four-hundred-foot-high cliffs and watched plumes of thin yellow smoke waft through the air. At various spots along the trails and edges of the cliffs, there were piles of offerings: *ti* leaves, woven coconut fronds, loaves of bread, hot dogs, bottles, cans of Spam. People leave them to incur the favor of Pele. The ancient Hawaiians believed that Pele, the goddess of the volcano, has the power not only to destroy with violent volcanic eruptions but also to create islands at her whim. Scientists cannot predict the timing or the exact magnitude of the volcanic eruptions.[28]

I understood now how many people become avid volcano watchers and professional volcanologists, obsessed with the enigma of this natural phenomenon. But the sulfurous vapors are pungent. Mark Twain once said, "The smell of sulpher (sic) is strong but not unpleasant to a sinner." Prone to asthma, I found it very unpleasant and had difficulty breathing. I was catching smoke, not paradise.

Paulette turned to me and said, "Well, we've seen the fiery lava and the smoking caldera. Awe inspiring, but what do we do now?"

"We get the hell out of here," I said.

---

28. *On May 3, 2018, Kilauea erupted, covering 2,400 acres in new lava. The summit belched fifteen thousand tons of sulfur dioxide each day, five times the amount as when we first set foot on the island.*

CHAPTER TWENTY-SIX

Paradise Attained

Aia no i ke ko a ke au.
Whichever way the current goes.
—ANCIENT HAWAIIAN PROVERB

We had island fever—we had to get off the rock. Our self-imposed exile in the middle of the Pacific was beginning to include periods of monotony; my wife and I felt too young to retire. We had bought our house at a propitious time when we were forty-three years old, desiring a quiet place where the sun shone every day, but John Donne's famous phrase now came to mind: "No man is an island entire of itself." We missed cultural events and museums. Living on an island can engender a spiritual state of mind, rather like living in an ashram, a hermitage, or a monastery. Like many who repair to temples, forests, or the slopes of the Himalayas, we had found refuge and rejuvenation, feeling we had escaped the confusion of the modern world. But it was my impression that Hawai'i was in danger of becoming a patchwork of suburban enclaves. I'd arrived a hundred years too late. A majority of islanders have forgotten traditional customs. The language is known, but, like Latin, only a few phrases are used regularly. And only about eight thousand islanders are fluent in Hawaiian while the rest rely on English and Pidgin.

Many small authentic eateries have closed, making room for trendy places and fast-food chains. Even the herd of wild donkeys from the area north of the airport had to be split up and moved to make way for more megaresorts. Like so many things over the years, they are seen as an impediment to progress.

Despite the fact that we had made good friends in our village and loved the place, we became acutely aware that we were not living in paradise. When we had first moved to the island, there was an old-style plantation cottage up the street from us, inhabited by a large extended Hawaiian family. The grandfather, who had a gray ponytail, frequently tended a fire out front in a long pit, the *imu*. In it the family would cook taro, vegetables, fish, and pork wrapped in banana leaves. But the old man moved away; things changed. The lot was frequently filled with cars, sometimes as many as twenty. At night we would hear screams—domestic abuse—and police officers would come every so often to haul someone off to jail. It would quiet down for a spell, and then the mysterious activity would resume—there always seemed to be something cooking. Finally a neighbor revealed the truth: "No more food in the *imu*," he explained. "They're cooking ice, methamphetamine." The terrible scourge of drugs is another devastating importation to the islands.

All in all, I started to feel this was not my idea of paradise. The phrase "No one wanders under palm trees unpunished," written by Goethe, came to mind.

We called our real estate agent, Valerie, who placed a "For Sale" sign in our front yard. To me it was a tombstone, a symbol of the impending end of our island life. The magic of the black of night enhances our senses; we lose our defenses and succumb to a spirit world. But human hearts can be like dark forests, and that night I dreamed the mythical night marchers walked into my bedroom. Then something was strangling the life out of me until I awoke, gasping for air and dripping in sweat. I had lost my *mana*.

I'm not prone to phantasmagorical fears, but I had once heard that there are ghosts in many of the houses in Hawai'i, and that to quiet them, one must make friends with them. I went outside, and the night was as silent as the flowers in our garden. I directed the yellow beam of my flashlight onto the sign and tore it out of the ground. Tears were streaming down my face as I dragged it into the carport. Then I heard from above a tap, tap, tap on the corrugated-iron roof. Rain came pouring down in buckets, a rarity on this part of the island. I remembered the old saying that raindrops are just the tears of angels crying.

The next morning at the breakfast table, my head hanging over a cup of Kona coffee, Paulette said, "No place is perfect." She suggested we put the house up for vacation rentals.

"That's it: share the aloha spirit," I said, brightening at the prospect as the Kona caffeine rush kicked in. Perhaps we could still live the island life during holidays.

On the other hand, with the ever-increasing population, maybe we *should* sell it, I thought, and sail a catamaran on a Polynesian voyage. "Remember that special little island a couple of weeks' sail south? I think it starts with the letter *M*?" I said.

"Moorea?" she said. The island is only twelve miles from her homeland, Tahiti; she knows the South Sea islands well.

"No."

"Maui?"

"That's only hours from here!"

"Mangareva? Maupiti?"

"Maybe it was an *H*?"

"Hiva Oa? Hikueru?"

"It might have started with an *F*?" I said, rather enjoying this goading game of dreaming of delightful islands.

"Fanning Island? Fatu Hiva? Fakarava? What's your favorite?"

"The one you're on, sweetie," I said.

With the prospect of leaving the island, another chapter of my life was closing—my dream ending—and our unavoidable mortality seemed closer.

Aloha, the divine breath of life, means hello, yes. And *aloha* is love. *Aloha* also means goodbye.

Epilogue

We put our house up for vacation rentals; we had family business to attend to, and we wanted to *haolefy* Will, have him finish high school in California. He was becoming such an island boy. We figured if he didn't get into the hustle-and-bustle life, he'd turn into a beach bum, something at which I was becoming an expert. Well, it didn't work. Upon graduation on the mainland, he chose the University of Hawai'i. He loved it. We continued to visit the islands whenever we could. It wasn't the same, but the aloha elixir, the spirit or *mana* of the volcanic hot spot, still soothed our souls.

One year, a week before Christmas, we'd rented out our house but at the last minute decided we needed an island hit. So Paulette and I checked into a condo near Diamond Head. Anthony was living nearby, as after college he'd landed an insurance job in Honolulu. On a Sunday afternoon, we went to Duke's to hear Henry Kapono play guitar and sing his island-style rock songs.

Christmas Eve, we attended the service at St. Augustine by-the-Sea, Father Damien's[29] church in Waikīkī at the end of Kalakaua Avenue, now a tourist road.

We struck up the hymn "For All the Saints," which seemed particularly relevant to the islands: "The golden evening brightens in the west;/ Soon, soon to faithful warriors comes their rest;/ Sweet is the calm of paradise the blessed."

After the evening service, we strolled past the statue of Duke Kahanamoku, my surfing hero, and along the seashore path all the way to the Ala Wai Harbor and into the Chart House. There, the owner Joey Cabell told us that he not only knew Duke but also won the Duke Kahanamoku Invitational surf contest in 1969. Over the dinner special, the trim and lively seventy-eight-year-old Joey told us, "You have to expand your sports. One can expand to another. For me, surfing evolved into sailing, canoe paddling, and then snowboarding in Aspen."

"We skied one hundred days last year," Yana, Joey's *wahine*, said to Paulette.

Joey pointed to the harbor in the direction of his custom-built forty-foot catamaran.[30] "Racing next week. I sailed her to Tahiti in ten days in 1975. And in between here and Lanai, I caught a 325-pound ahi, still the state record."

"That's *really* expanding your sports," I said.

---

29. *On October 11, 2009, Father Damien—the Belgian priest who went to help the lepers on Moloka'i, and who after twelve years was afflicted with Hansen's disease ("I am one of them now," he said)—was canonized.*

30. *Joey's boat has the same name as the sixty-two-foot traditional Polynesian canoe Hōkūle'a, which has sailed around the world, captained by Nainoa Thompson with the Polynesian Voyaging Society, spreading a message of mālama honua: caring for the earth.*

On another evening, we went to the Halekulani Hotel for the sunset hula show at House Without a Key. That night, the blonde Lauren Kealohilani Matsumoto, Miss Hawai'i 2011, swung her hula hips to the rhythm of the band by the seashore. She walked barefoot by our table and said, "I'm Hawai'i State House representative from Mililani and a sixth-generation Hawaiian. My family's farm still operates today." Only in Hawai'i do we have beautiful hula-dancing politicians!

After watching the lovely hula show, we walked up the beach, careful not to get wet from the crashing waves, to the Moana Hotel for dinner underneath the giant banyan tree. The press was everywhere as Barrack Obama was on the island.

At the Beach Bar, the band's singer said, "*E komo mai*, welcome, our shaka president." The *hapa haole/hapa popolo* appeared on the television above the seaside bar, flashing the shaka sign, shaking his extended pinkie and thumb in what is known in Hawai'i to be a friendly gesture.

We ran into Kalani, one of our former surf instructors. He said, "He went to Punahou. One president and two saints made in Hawai'i in just a few years."

"Two saints?" Will asked.

"Moddah Marianne,[31] yah," Kalani said.

"Mother," Will corrected. College student.

Paulette nodded in agreement. "She worked with Father Damien and treated lepers for thirty-five years and established hospitals."

Anthony, who had once chosen Robert Louis Stevenson as his subject for a presentation in English literature class, said, "Stevenson saw Mother Marianne and the other sisters and wrote, 'Beauty springing from the breast of pain!'"

---

31. *The "Blessed Marianne Cope of Moloka'i" was canonized by the Vatican on October 21, 2012.*

"Very poetic," I said, impressed and proud of my sons on this Christmas Eve.

With the holidays, no rental cars were left on the island, a fact we discovered after making a dozen phone calls and walking the back alleys in search of anything with wheels to get us over to the North Shore. Finally, in a weedy lot strewn with rusted cars, we got the last rent-a-wreck. As we sputtered down the H-1, it rained so hard that puddle water sloshed through the floorboards of the Jeep. With no windows in the back, our sons covered themselves with towels as we wound around the curves of Waimea Bay and then Pūpūkea, where Elvis once lived. Ten minutes after we checked into a condo by Turtle Bay, we lost electricity. As we walked up to a nearby hotel to sniff about for food, a man holding a flashlight said, "The whole island's blacked out. Downtown, airport, everywhere. Bad electrical grid."

After a candlelit dinner, our family stood on the patio, listening to the waves crashing on the shore. With no lights, the stargazing was seamless. I couldn't help but reflect that perhaps Hawai'i is the most beautiful place in the world. I thought of Robert Louis Stevenson's last words written in Hawai'i: "If anyone desire such old-fashioned things as lovely scenery, quiet, pure air, clear sea water, good food, and heavenly sunsets hung out before his eyes over the Pacific . . ."

"Perhaps we should spend our retirement years here," Paulette said.

"A reinvention of the paradise years," I said.

A new adventure was beginning.

—*W. C., Hawai'i, 2019*

Glossary

'a'ama—black edible crab that runs over shore rocks

'āina—land, earth

'āina haole—foreign land, mainland United States

'āina momona—rich, fertile land

akamai—smart, clever

aku—bonito fish

ahua—God, spirit, idol

alaia—thin surfboard of breadfruit or *koa* wood

ali'i—chief, king, queen, monarch, aristocrat

aloha—love, affection, mercy, compassion, greetings, farewell

aloha nui loa—very much love

ama—outrigger float

Aotearoa—land of the long white cloud, Maori for New Zealand

'aumakua—family or personal spirits

auwe—Oh! Oh dear! Alas! Too bad! Goodness!

'awa—kava, *Piper methysticum*: a plant native to the Pacific isles

brah—pal or friend (Pidgin)

buggah—guy, friend, or pest (Pidgin)

cockaroach—to steal or sneak away with (Pidgin)

da kine—(literally, "the kind") Hawaiian mental telepathy

e komo mai—come in, welcome

ha—to breathe, exhale

haka—Maori ritualized bravado of contortions and jesting

Hakka—Chinese group from the foothills of China proper

hapa—portion, fragment, part, half, of mixed blood

hale—house, building

hale ali'i—house of the chiefs or royal families

hana hou—to do again, repeat

haole—foreigner (literally "without breath")

haolefy—(slang) to turn into a *haole*

hau'oli—happy, glad, gay, joyful

Havaiki/Hawaiki—homeland (throughout much of Polynesia)

he'e—octopus, squid

he'e nalu—surfing (literally "wave sliding")

heiau—shrine, stone platform, place of worship

hele—to go, come, walk

hilahila—bashful, shy, ashamed, embarrassed

ho'i mai—come back

Hōkūle'a—a navigational star, probably Arcturus

hongi—a Maori embrace in which two people touch noses

honi—to kiss, a kiss

honu—turtle

huhu—angry, indignant, mad

huli—to turn, reverse; to curl over, as a breaker; to change

humuhumunukunukuapua'a—triggerfish

'iako—outrigger boom

'ilima—native shrubs bearing yellow, orange, or green flowers

imu—underground oven, food cooked in an *imu*

'iolani—royal hawk, native of Hawai'i

ipo—sweetheart

ka'ai—sennit casket, protective cloth wrap

kahuna—priest, sorcerer, expert in any profession

kakou—we (inclusive, for three or more)

kala—money (short for *kala dala*, "dollar money")

kalua—to bake in the ground oven, baked

kama'āina—native-born, from the land

kāmau—to keep on, continue, persevere

kana ipo—his or her sweetheart

kanaka maoli—full-blooded Hawaiian person

kapa—tapa, made from bark; formerly clothes of any kind

kapakahi—one-sided, crooked, lopsided, sideways, askew

kapu—prohibited, forbidden, no trespassing

kaukau—food, a slang term similar to *chow*

keiki—child, small young person, children

"Ke Kali Nei Au"—the Hawaiian wedding song

kiawe—algaroba tree

koa—the largest of native forest trees

kolohe—rascal, mischievous

kou—a tree with ovate leaves and tubular orange flowers

kumara—sweet potato (Maori)

laho—scrotum

Lalamilo—a district/division of land on the west side of Hawai'i

laulau—food wrapped in leaves and steamed

lele wa'a—whale sharks (literally "flying canoes")

liliko'i—passion fruit

limu—seaweed

lolo—stupid, crazy

Lono—one of the four major gods or spirits

luau—feast

mahalo—thank you

mahi-mahi—dolphinfish, a game fish popular for food

mahu—homosexual, of either sex; hermaphrodite

mai'a—banana

mai tai—good (Tahitian)

maka—eye

makahiki—year, ancient festival

malihini—newcomer

mana—spiritual power

manako—mango

mano—shark

manu—bird

maoli—native Hawaiian, Polynesian

Maori—New Zealand native

mauna—mountain, mountainous region

Mauna Kea—highest mountain on Hawai'i

mele—song, anthem, chant, or poem

Mele Kalikimaka—Merry Christmas

mikana—papaya

milo—tree found on the coasts

moana—ocean, open sea

musubi—block of rice with Spam and seaweed wrapping

nahenahe—soft, sweet, melodious

nani—beauty, beautiful, pretty, glorious, splendid

niho—tooth

niuhi—man-eating shark

nohu pinao—turkey fish with poisonous spines

noni   Indian mulberry

nui—big, large, great, important

'ohana—family, relative, kin group, related

'ōhi'a—a species of tree found on islands in the Pacific

'okole—buttocks

olo—long surfboard, to saw, to resound

'ono—delicious, tasty, savory; to relish, crave

ono kine—delicious kind (slang)

onolicious—delicious (Hawaiian combined with English, slang)

'opihi—limpets

'opu—belly, stomach

pahoehoe smooth, unbroken type of lava

paka lolo—marijuana

Pākē—China, Chinese

palupalu—weak, soft, flexible, tender, supple

paniolo—cowboy

panipani—to close; coition and to practice such (vulgar)

pau—finished, done

pau hana—quitting time

Pele—the volcano goddess, lava flow, volcanic eruption

pikake—Arabian jasmine

piko—navel

pilau—rotten, putrid, spoiled, foul

poi—mashed taro

poisson cru—raw fish (French), popular in Tahiti

poke—to slice or cut into pieces, as fish or wood

Poli-'ahu—snow goddess of Mauna Kea

pono—goodness, righteousness, well-being, excellence

popolo—a black nightshade; modern slang for black people

pua—flower, blossom

pua'a—pig, hog, pork

pua ko—stem and tassel of sugarcane

pueo—owl

puhi—eel

puka—hole

Punti—A population group from the lowlands of China

pupu—appetizer, hors d'oeuvre, or general name for shells

pupule—crazy, insane, wild

tako—octopus (Japanese)

ti—also *ki*, a woody plant in the lily family native to Asia

tiare—gardenia flower native to Tahiti

ule—penis

'ulu—breadfruit

ulua—crevalle, jack, or pompano fish

va'a—canoe (Tahitian)

vog—black volcanic smoke clouds, a play on "smog"

wa'a—canoe

waha nui—big mouth

wahine—female, wife

wai momi—water of pearls, former name of Pearl Harbor

waina—wine

Waipi'o—valley on the northeast side of Hawai'i (literally "Curved Water")

wikiwiki—fast, speedy

List of Illustrations

Acknowledgments

Many thanks to the editors: Jill Liebster, Mark Miller, my brother Barnaby Conrad III, my late father Barnaby Conrad Jr., and especially my wife Paulette Conrad. Adam Gomolin, Avalon Radys, and Elena Stofle at Inkshares. Many *mahalos* to George Robertson for teaching me about the Big Island's history, Harry Wishard for his commissioned oil painting for the cover and for the photos of Ernest Hemingway hunting in Hawaii, Hope Cromwell Hopkins for the use of her old photos, the Puako Historical Society and John Hoover for inspiring facts, Tom Morgan for design, Will James Conrad for graphic concepts, Anthony Conrad for financial advice, Bernard and Marie-Alice Nogues, John Marrow and Cynthia Ho, Guy and Linda Startsman, Maggie Haunani Woods, Budd and Peg Schmeltz, Anthony Lee, Paul Theroux, Forrest Furman, Jimmy Buffett, Kelly Slater, Randy Rarick, Guy Steele, the Rutgers family, and the Callender family for their warm *aloha* to the islands.

Grand Patrons

Alexandra Stick

Anthony Chan Conrad

Barnaby Conrad III

Brian Ross

Bunnie Crichton

Dana S. Jones

Duncan A. Chapman

Ned and Dianna Lawrence

Henry C. Gibson III

Joan Sadler

Juliette McDowell

Lopekana

Margaret H. Woods

Mark C. McDowell

Martin Muller

Matthew K. McDowell

Michael Canseco

Michael O'Toole

Michael Slater

Paula H. Gibson

Ralph D. Lewis

Randy Ferguson

Sandra Vega

Tani Conrad

Theresa A. Lum

Thomas H. Stick

Tony Guzzardo

Walton Logan

William J. Conrad

Wyman C. Harris